A Decade of Central African Republic

A Decade of Central African Republic

Politics, Economy and Society 2009–2018

By

Andreas Mehler

BRILL

LEIDEN | BOSTON

Library of Congress Control Number: 2020941107

Typeface for the Latin, Greek, and Cyrillic scripts: "Brill". See and download: brill.com/
brill-typeface.

ISBN 978-90-04-43599-5 (paperback)
ISBN 978-90-04-43600-8 (e-book)

This book is printed on acid-free paper and produced in a sustainable manner.

Contents

Preface

When I first touched ground in the Central African Republic (CAR) in February 1993, this was after the first – manipulated and annulled – multi-party elections since independence and ahead of the first free elections, which brought Ange-Félix Patassé to power. I had a modest role in preparing those elections, and later an equally modest role in the international election observation mission. Those were exciting times, with many hopes, but already many doubts as to the course the country would take. Patassé represented "the savannah" – the first president of the Republic not to have come from the somewhat privileged "river" zone.

When I wrote my first yearbook article it was for the German *Afrika Jahrbuch* in 1995 (covering 1994). I had to report how Patassé had started a witch-hunt against followers of his predecessor, the "civilized" military leader André Kolingba. From there on, I had the opportunity to write yearly overview articles on this country; this has been one of my tasks now for a quarter of a century.

In the meantime, we turned the *Afrika Jahrbuch* into the *Africa Yearbook* and in 2005 (covering 2004) I started to write my country chapter for the new outlet. The year 2004 saw the gradual establishment of François Bozizé, a year after he had toppled his former ally Patassé with the help of so-called "liberators". These combatants, most of Chadian origin, began racketeering among the inhabitants of Bangui – a precursor of worse things to come.

When Brill Publishers offered me the opportunity to write a preface for *A Decade of Central African Republic (2009–2018)* earlier this year I gladly accepted the offer. This booklet now covers those last ten years, which were – above all – particularly violent. In the early chapters of this collection, i.e. before the appearance of the somewhat coordinated Séléka rebellion (in September 2012) one can read that peace did certainly not prevail in CAR. In fact, several parts of the country were already witnessing repeated skirmishes, among rebel movements but also with the Chadian army – though this was largely ignored by a broader public. Some of the veterans of political life died in this period (long-term opponent Abel Goumba in 2009, Kolingba in 2010 and Patassé in 2012). They had represented the older fault-lines within the country: the area around the capital Bangui (profiting from rather good education facilities and public investment) versus the aspiring, fairly well-populated and fertile (north)west. But from 2012 onwards, actors from the strongly neglected north-east made their aspirations known, and a Christian–Muslim divide could no longer be ignored. CAR became a focus country for peace initiatives and peacekeeping operations, not least because of this juxtaposition with potentially wider implications. However, local constellations between powerful actors (and also vulnerable groups) always varied strongly, which every year is what makes it so difficult to write a consistent chapter with a main storyline.

It is admittedly also a sad exercise to write every year mostly about war and bloodshed, and rarely about reconciliation or material progress. The inhabitants of CAR merit a better fate. I did not expect this course of events when I started my chronicle. But I would certainly also not have expected the explosion of scholarly works on CAR in this period. In the 1990s, only very few colleagues took an interest in CAR; this has changed dramatically and much for the better. This booklet contains a select bibliography of works on CAR published since 2009 which might give a first orientation to those who would seek more analytical depth.

I want to thank the entire team at Brill (Bas, Franca, Joed, but also the three subsequent language editors who took care of the approximate English of a non-native speaker) for doing an excellent job in all aspects surrounding the publication of the complex work that is the *Africa Yearbook*.

Andreas Mehler
Freiburg, March 2020

Central African Republic in 2009

The political atmosphere of the somewhat promising end of 2008 could not be maintained for long. Few of the concessions made by President Bozizé during the inclusive political dialogue (IPD) forum were eventually implemented. New armed encounters all over the country marked the year, while the president's camp was already preparing for the 2010 elections. Rebel movements fought mainly for material gains, but had also good reason to suspect the regime of not fulfilling its earlier promises and some real grievances related to the blatant disregard of minority group rights. The export-oriented economy (diamonds, timber) suffered from the global economic downturn.

Domestic Politics

President Bozizé dissolved the government on 18 January and immediately reappointed Prime Minister Touadéra the following day. His newly formed *'government of national unity'*, meant to include representatives of both opposition parties and rebel movements, fell far short of expectations. Only second-rank members of those contesting parties made their entry into the government and occupied mostly medium-weight positions. This was particularly true for the representative of the opposition alliance, the 'Union des Forces Vives de la Nation' (UFVN), André Nalke Dorogo, who was made minister of public health. His party, the 'Mouvement pour la Libération du Peuple Centrafricain' (MLPC) excluded him from its ranks after he accepted this position. Moïse Kotaye, contested leader of the 'Front Patriotique pour le Progrès' (FPP), supposed to represent the second opposition alliance simply called 'Autres Partis', was made minister of small and medium-sized companies. His participation in government was also dismissed by those he was

© KONINKLIJKE BRILL NV, LEIDEN, 2020 | DOI:10.1163/9789004436008_002

deemed to represent. Equally second-rank were those ministers representing the armed movements, such as François Naoyama of the 'Armée Populaire pour la Restauration de la Démocratie' (APRD) and Djomo Didou of the 'Union des Forces Démocratiques pour le Rassemblement' (UFDR), who were made ministers of the environment and housing respectively.

Key ministries were still held by staunch *presidential supporters*. In particular, Cyriaque Gonda, leader of the 'Parti National pour un Centrafrique Nouveau' (PNCN), saw his powers increased and was now made state minister for communication, civic affairs, national reconciliation and the follow-up of the IPD. Sylvain Ndoutingaï continued to manage the ministry of mines, energy and water, and Col. Anicet Parfait Mbaye the ministry of transport and civil aviation. Sylvain Maliko headed the plan, economy and international cooperation department. Former chief of staff Gen. Antoine Gambi became foreign minister. As the opposition had criticised the fact that Bozizé combined his function of head of state with that of minister of defence, he introduced a cosmetic move promoting his son Francis from junior minister within the ministry to full defence minister, while preserving his control over the strategic post. Hopes that Bozizé would share substantial parts of his power were therefore futile.

Obviously related to the ensuing frustration were new outbursts of *violence*. In fact, serious setbacks in the peace process were recorded, despite some progress in 2008 with the signature of a global peace accord by most of the main rebel movements. Only Zacharia Damane's UFDR, dominated by ethnic Gula, respected the peace agreement with government forces. However, it came increasingly under attack in its stronghold of Birao (north-east) from competing Kara militias, leading to serious confrontations at its Birao base in June on two separate occasions. Four UFDR combatants were killed against about 15 of the attackers. After UN mediation (1–4 July), the UFDR agreed to leave the destroyed and deserted town for its base in Tiringoulou. Earlier skirmishes between armed groups occurred in mid-January in Ndélé (Bamingui-Bangoran prefecture). In retaliation, the armed forces attacked the nearby village of Sokoumba and killed at least 18 male civilians, including the village chief. In February, an armed group attacked the prison of Bossembelé, 160 km north of Bangui, freed all prisoners and seized weaponry and ammunition. Responsibility for the attack was claimed by the newly created 'Convention des Patriotes pour la Justice et la Paix' (CPJP), led by the ominous political entrepreneur Charles Massi, who had agreed to become UFDR coordinator (i.e. political spokesperson) the year before.

Subsequently, CPJP was involved in further attacks in the northeast, including in Ndélé in June. *Retaliation* by government forces reportedly caused the displacement of 5,000 civilians. The army also allegedly killed 30 civilians during the operation. The CPJP stayed outside any peace framework through the entire year. Massi was arrested by Chadian authorities when trying to cross the border from Chad into CAR to join CPJP troops based near the border, but was released in July for unknown reasons. After a short occupation of Ndélé by about 400 CPJP troops on 26 November (11 people were killed), the town was recaptured by the army two days later. Massi was arrested by the Chadian army again in mid-December and was then handed over to the CAR authorities, who transferred him to the prison in Bossembélé where he was allegedly tortured (and killed, though his death was not officially confirmed).

The *north and north-west* were equally theatres of combat. In late February, rebels attacked a gendarmerie post in Bataganfo, 500 km north of Bangui, stealing weaponry and equipment. Two armed groups claimed to have staged the attack, the 'Front Démocratique du Peuple Centrafricain' (FDPC) and the 'Mouvement des Libérateurs Centrafricains pour la Justice' (MLCJ). Both organisations had suspended their participation in the peace process. However, on 31 May, MLCJ leader Abakar Sabone returned to Bangui and agreed to work within the framework of the peace process. On 3 July, FDPC leader Abdoulaye Miskine signed the Libreville peace accord on the sidelines of the AU summit in Sirte (Libya), but later (on 2 October) declared that he would step out of the peace process, sparking a split within his movement. The APRD, though officially sticking to the peace process, was involved in several incidents. Stockbreeders accused local traders in Paoua of selling 170 cattle that had been stolen by bandits ten days earlier. The ensuing clashes left 22 dead and 52 injured. Only a few days later a top representative of the cattle breeders, Soule Garga, was killed by APRD rebels. Jean-Jacques Démafouth, coordinator of the APRD, thereafter replaced the local APRD commander as he feared losing some of the existing sympathy of the local population.

Chadian rebel leader Baba Laddé, opposed to the Déby regime in N'Djaména and initially allied to the APRD, operated with his men in the APRD strongholds around Kaga Bandoro, claiming to fight the dreaded 'Zaraguina' highway robbers. He was declared persona non grata in October, arrested and deported. His 'Front Populaire pour le Redressement' (FPR) and *Chadian forces* had clashed in the border town of Sido on 3 October. Laddé's supporters now threatened to wage a 'jihad' against the government and the peacekeepers of CEEAC's 'Mission de consolidation de la paix' (MICOPAX). This added to the more and more religiously loaded confrontations Bozizé had with groups of Muslim origin. In November, two French aid workers were kidnapped near Birao by rebel fighters who apparently belonged to the 'Mouvement National du Salut de la Patrie' (MNSP), a break-away faction of the MLCJ under hardliner Hassan Ousman, who fell out with Sabone and reportedly took with him most of the fighters.

The government authorised the Ugandan army to conduct military operations on CAR territory together with Southern Sudanese and Congolese troops following repeated attacks and looting by the Ugandan rebel movement *Lord's Resistance Army* (LRA) in the southeast (around Obo and Mboki), which displaced an estimated 4,500 civilians. The Ugandan army was subsequently reported to have rescued 100 kidnapped children and young adults, killing one senior and four junior commanders and capturing a senior LRA commander; 46 LRA fighters would have surrendered to Southern Sudanese forces. Nevertheless, LRA attacks continued in late November, when 24 people were abducted and 11 killed in new attacks. Additionally, confrontations between ethnic Sango and Ngbubu made more than 500 inhabitants of Mobaye-Banga (South) flee over the River Oubangui into DR Congo in September, where both groups cohabited peacefully.

In the light of these events, any *disarmament*, demobilisation, and reintregration (DDR) process looked intrinsically unrealistic. After some preparatory work, Bozizé nevertheless officially launched the DDR programme in Paoua (north-west) after provisional lists of ex-combatants had been submitted to the UN. Initial funds of $ 4 m were released from the UN Peacebuilding Fund. In addition, a new round of collection of small and light weapons was launched shortly afterwards. A three-year plan to disarm 6,000–10,000 fighters was announced in December, but apart from a couple of information meetings little had been achieved by year's end.

Without tangible success in the DDR process, it looked difficult to conduct peaceful *presidential elections* in 2010. Bozizé nevertheless prepared his re-election by all possible means. His 'Convention Kwa Na Kwa', hitherto a platform of movements supporting the president, formally registered as a political party (simply 'Kwa Na Kwa', literally 'work, nothing but work') after an inaugurating meeting in Boali on 29 August. It later held a first congress in M'baiki (13 November). Gonda's PNCN reiterated its support for Bozizé.

The National Assembly adopted a new *electoral code* after controversy over the nomination process of the independent electoral commission ('Commission Electorale Indépendante'; CEI). The two opposition alliances, which had boycotted the vote, suspended their participation in the selection process of the commissioners, while the Constitutional Court had declared some provisions of the text anti-constitutional. Pierre Buyoya, Burundi's former president and chief mediator in the IPD, former archbishop Paulin (the head of the National Council for Mediation) and the new Special Representative of the UN Secretary General (SRSG), Sahle-Work Zewde, negotiated a compromise. A somewhat modified code was promulgated on 2 October and pastor Joseph Binguimale was subsequently elected chairman of the commission by a majority of its 30 members. Binguimale worked hard to respect the deadline of the initial electoral calendar, i.e. holding elections in April 2010. Whereas the minister of territorial administration had announced in April that voters' lists would have to be set up entirely anew, because those used in 2005 were said to have been destroyed, Binguimale announced in December that he had 'found' the lists and it was now a simple matter of updating them. This announcement reinforced looming suspicions that the government would use manipulated voter lists.

Former president Ange Félix Patassé came back to Bangui (via Libya) from his exile in Togo in October and met with Bozizé on 9 November. He still enjoyed support within the MLPC, the *main opposition party*, although a party congress had excluded him on 13 June for "not respecting the line of the party". Supporters were not allowed to welcome Patassé at the airport. His return and announcement that he would stand in the 2010 polls challenged the ambitions of Martin Ziguélé, former prime minister and new party chairman, who had been Bozizé's most serious contender in the 2005 elections. However, on 31 December the Supreme Court confirmed an earlier court ruling that Ziguélé was the rightful leader of the MLPC.

On 15 June, the ICC officially confirmed the charges against Jean-Pierre Bemba, DR Congo's former vice president, for *crimes against humanity* committed in CAR in 2002–3 when Patassé had called upon him for help. The 'Fédération Internationale de Droits de l'Homme' continued to demand the issuing of arrest warrants by the ICC against Patassé (and Miskine) for the same crimes. This was clearly not supported by the authorities, because Patassé was an obvious ally of Bozizé against Ziguélé – at least for the moment.

Veteran politician Abel *Goumba* died on 11 May. He was a central figure in national politics in the 1960s and 1990s, but had lost influence in recent years, although he headed a government of national reconciliation under Bozizé in 2003. Goumba held the position of National Mediator until his death. He was succeeded in this position by former archbishop Pomodimo.

Foreign Affairs

The death of the highly influential Omar Bongo Ondimba, President of *Gabon*, had repercussions in CAR. Bongo had time and again brokered agreements between the various conflicting parties of the country. It was not expected that his son Ali, the new president, would be as committed to regional diplomacy as was his father. The local UN peacebuilding office became increasingly active. It was renamed 'Bureau intégré des Nations Unies pour la consolidation de la paix en Centrafrique' under the new SRSG, the experienced Ethiopian female career diplomat, Sahle-Work Zewde.

When the EUFOR Chad/CAR mission was officially terminated on 15 March, the UN Mission in the Central African Republic and Chad (MINURCAT by its French acronym) had to take over. The *UN mission* was – in principle – strengthened in advance on 14 January by UN Security Council resolution 1861 and authorised to total 5,200 military personnel, 25 military liaison officers and 300 police officers. The mandate was extended until 15 March 2010. Finland and Sweden, which had participated in EUFOR, agreed to be part of 'MINURCAT 2'. The EU Council issued statements of satisfaction with the overall success of the EUFOR mission. Because of delays in deployment of additional troops, France agreed to keep its EUFOR contingent in place for some additional weeks. However, like EUFOR, the UN mission was focusing largely on Chad and only superficially on north-eastern CAR, with only about 500 soldiers operating on Central African soil. In April, UN assistant secretary general for peacekeeping, Edmond Mulet, admitted that MINURCAT lacked soldiers and equipment essential to its mission. At the end of the year, UN peacekeepers were deployed to Sam Ouandja in the north-east, when Sudanese rebels threatened to attack that village. The UN's peacebuilding commission remained active in the CAR and concretised its plans with a strategic framework paper adopted on 9 June and a second mission to the country in December. APRD rebels, however, refused the commission's delegation access to Paoua.

CEEAC's MICOPAX, which had taken over from a similar CEMAC force as the sub-regional complement of peacekeeping troops, operated in the central and western part of the country. The allegedly 'arrogant' Chadian contingent met with suspicion from the population of the capital Bangui (as had been the case with all former regional peacekeeping units of Chadian origin since 1997). The mission built barracks in several cities and partly handed them over to the national armed forces. Under French pressure, the reluctant CEEAC agreed to supply 31 additional military observers to oversee the DDR process. They arrived in mid-December.

Bozizé visited *China* between 9 and 15 September and called on Chinese investors to step up their interests in CAR, notably in communications and mining. Presidents Hu Jintao and Bozizé signed an agreement on technological and economic cooperation.

In January the regime annoyed *France* with the appointment of controversial businessman Saifee Durbar (of Indo-Pakistani origin) to deputy minister for foreign affairs. The move was meant to give Durbar diplomatic immunity in order to escape prosecution in London and Paris. He was dismissed from his position in June, obviously under French pressure, and extradited from the United Kingdom to France on 2 December. He was arrested on charges of fraud.

Socioeconomic Developments

GDP was forecast to grow by only 2%, a slowdown compared with the 2.2% calculated for 2008. The global financial crisis had a direct negative impact on both major *export commodities*. Timber exports dropped by 38%, and the value of exported diamonds, in previous years making up for some 50% of exports, declined by 27%. A long-awaited new mining code, aimed at creating more transparency in the sector, was adopted in April, but fell short of expectations and increased the tax for foreign mining companies. It was feared that it made the investment climate even more unattractive.

The 2009 *budget*, approved by the National Assembly in late 2008, was highly expansionary with a 24% increase in spending. Total revenue was set to increase by 20.3%. The budget was based on an assumption of real GDP growth of 4.5% in the calendar year and could soon be declared unrealistic. The government nevertheless worked on ameliorated domestic revenue collection and improved management of public expenditure. Domestic debt was thereby reportedly reduced by a significant CFAfr 12 bn. The IMF was, on the whole, satisfied with the implementation of the PRGF, particularly with fiscal performance, and extended the facility for a further six months into mid-2010. In July, CAR attained the completion point under the HIPC initiative, the precondition for large-scale *debt* relief. Multilateral debt was, in fact, reduced by $ 578 m and the total debt owed to Paris Club creditors declined from $ 59.3 m to $ 3.7 m in 2009. The IMF expressed its hope that the freed resources would be used to meet some of the MDGs where the CAR was far behind schedule. On 29 December, the National Assembly approved the 2010 budget, increased by 7.9% to CFAfr 184.6 bn, with 42% of the budget planned to be covered by outside support.

Reports multiplied about growing *malnutrition* and a rise in related illnesses in diamond-producing areas around Nola and Boda. The already poor standards of cassava-based nutrition could not be met by dismissed miners. According to UNICEF, 700,000 children below the age of five were severely malnourished. Extreme *poverty* was cited as a cause, with six out of ten people living on less than \$ 1.25 a day. Torrential rainfall led to *flooding* in Bangui in July and a substantial loss of housing and property.

The number of IDPs declined to 108,000 by February but, following the numerous new outbursts of violence, rose again to an estimated 162,000 in October. Among these, 73,000 people had earlier returned to their villages of origin, but were not able to build a sustainable basis of subsistence as violence continued. Refugees in neighbouring Cameroon and Chad numbered about 64,000 and 74,000 respectively.

A severe crisis affected the *Catholic Church*. Vatican officials had criticised the local clergy for living a double life, i.e. frequently having a wife and family. The bishop of Bossangoa announced his retirement in May, only to be followed by the country's archbishop Pomodimo. Both resignations were accepted by the Holy See and an apostolic administrator was appointed without consultation with the local hierarchy. This led to the surprising announcement of strike action by the country's priests on 27 May, suspended only the next day.

Central African Republic in 2010

Any achievements attained during 50 years of independence were difficult to show when the country officially celebrated the anniversary belatedly, not on 13 August, but on 1 December, the date when the legendary founding father of the Republic had declared autonomy within the 'Communauté Française' in 1958. Domestic politics were marked by continued clashes in the north-east and by haphazard preparations for national elections, which eventually had to be postponed to 2011. The insecurity that was prevalent on nearly all the country's borders dominated foreign policy activities, with the UN peacekeeping mission closing down two months before the announced elections. Some movement developed in the mining sector, which had still not returned to pre-war levels.

Domestic Politics

Early in the year, concerns about the government's management of the peace process (started with a peace agreement in July 2008 and followed by the 'Dialogue Politique Inclusif' [DPI] in December of that year) were raised in various quarters. On 16 January, the family of Charles Massi, chairman of the armed movement 'Convention des Patriotes pour la Justice et la Paix' (CPJP), alleged that he had died in custody on 8 January following torture after having been handed over by Chadian forces to the CAR authorities in late December 2009. Massi had been a minister under both Patassé and Bozizé and had run as presidential candidate in the 2005 elections. He was a controversial figure, straddling both civil and armed opposition. His assumed assassination nevertheless sent shock-waves throughout the political class. In mid-August, the public prosecutor announced that an official investigation had found no evidence that Massi had been handed over to the CAR authorities, and declared his official status as 'missing'. Massi's family rejected these findings and called for an international inquiry. The CPJP, the only movement of relevance that had refused to enter the peace process so far, continued its armed rebellion after Massi's *alleged death*. In the north-eastern region of Ndélé, *clashes* between the CPJP and the army in April led to at least ten rebels being killed. Even more challenging was the situation in the Vakaga préfecture: in mid-July the CPJP raided the provincial capital, Birao, but had to withdraw after a counter-attack by the army. The official death toll was 13. Bozizé appointed Major-General André Mazi as the new army chief in early October. Subsequently, the CPJP was driven out of the mining town of Yalinga, but then took the nearby town of Ippy, which was retaken by the army at the end of the month. On 6 September, five ministers visited Birao for a ceremony of reconciliation between the Arab, Gula, Hausa, Kara, Sara and Yulu groups living in the area. After the withdrawal of UN troops in November, the army reinforced its garrison in Birao to about 150 troops, but it was attacked on 24 November by the CPJP, who took control of the city for nearly a week. When the army retook the city in a fierce battle (with 71 officially declared dead), the rebels claimed that the army had had Chadian support, which was denied by the government.

Slow progress in implementing the DPI decisions was reported by the Follow-up Committee on 29 September. Of a total of 116 recommendations, 43 were fully implemented and 15 only partially. A new attempt to make progress in a futile *DDR* programme started in February, only to be stalled a few days later when Jean-Jacques Demafouth, political leader of the 'Armée Populaire pour la restauration de la République et la Démocratie' (APRD) and vice chairman of the DDR steering committee, and Bozizé's political adviser, Dieudonné Stanislas Mbangot, could not agree on payment modalities for the food allowance for DDR candidates. The entire year saw only limited progress, despite massive external support for the associated security sector reform. The UN Peacebuilding Commission granted $ 20 m in January to support projects focused on security sector reform, economic recovery and the rule of law.

Equally unresolved was the crisis in the south-east brought about by the intrusion of the formerly Ugandan-based *Lord's Resistance Army* (LRA). In early January, the Ugandan army claimed to have killed a senior LRA commander in the Haut-Mbomou province, but this did not impact strongly on its fighting power. In February, an LRA commando force attacked the mining town of Nzacko, close to Bangassou, killing civilians, looting and taking hostages. The Ugandan authorities believed that LRA leader Joseph Kony himself was in the CAR. He narrowly avoided capture near Obo in October. The LRA attacks spread towards the north, with raids on Tiroungoulou and Ouanda-Djallé. Local self-defence committees had meanwhile organised in the north-east, not least to defend communities against official anti-poaching militia. The rebel movement 'Union des Forces Démocratiques pour le Rassemblement' (UFDR) – at peace with the government – also fought the LRA. It was feared that the need for self-defence could become a strong argument for the delay of the DDR process. The reluctance of ex-rebels to disarm was probably also motivated by the prospect of losing control over mining sites. The Ugandan army operated with an estimated 7,000 troops from bases in Obo, Mboki, Zémio, Dembia, Djemah and Sam Ouandja. When they left Sam Ouandja, UFDR rebels took control of local diamond mining. LRA attacks displaced 32,000 people, 6,000 of them crossing the Oubangui River to the DRC.

The *preparation for national elections* suffered many setbacks. In January, the opposition withdrew from the 'Commission Électorale Indépendante' (CEI), claiming that its chairman had sided with the ruling party and local committees would have been created illegally. After a mission by the National Council for Mediation under Bangui's former archbishop Paulin Pomodimo, a new arrangement was signed on 13 February, *inter alia* permitting opposition movements to replace some of their representatives within the Commission and dissolving the local electoral committees. On 24 February, the CEI proposed an election calendar, fixing the first round of presidential elections for 18 April and the second for 23 May. Only one day later, Bozizé unilaterally set 25 April as the date for the first round of the elections. Both dates were unrealistic and most opposition movements asked for a suspension. Subsequently, Bozizé had to announce new dates (16 May/13 June), slightly over-lapping with the end of the current mandates of both the president and parliament (11 June). The civilian opposition and armed move-ments threatened to boycott the polls. After emergency talks, Bozizé postponed the elections indefinitely, but he received widespread support in all political camps for an extension of the mandates of both himself and the National Assembly. This necessitated a consti-tutional amendment, which was passed on 10 May. On 19 May, more than 30,000 people took to the streets of Bangui and expressed their approval of the postponement. A new timetable was proposed by the CEI in July (first round 24 October), which expressed the hope that organisational, security and funding issues would have been resolved by then. Bozizé overruled this by fixing a new date for late January 2011, which was accepted by the opposition in August. Voter registration was based on an overhaul of the old 2005 register and produced up to 1.8 m registered voters, an estimated 70%–75% of the population being of voting age. The list of candidates for the leg-islative elections was published on 13 December; about 70% of the 889 candidates were put forward by registered political parties. The rest were 'independents', mostly affiliated to Bozizé or Patassé.

The *opposition* was in a phase of re-orientation as a result of problems within the two most important groupings. Former state president and leader of the 'Rassemblement Démocratique Centrafricain' (RDC), André Kolingba, died in Paris on 7 February. The 'Mouvement pour la Libération du Peuple Centrafricain' (MLPC) remained split between a majority supporting former prime minister and party president Martin Ziguélé and those supporting former state president Ange-Félix Patassé. Both politicians were targeted by the regime. The government announced on 13 March that it had foiled a planned coup d'état against Bozizé, alluding to a role having been played by Patassé, who denied any involvement. In early May, Ziguélé was the victim of a temporary travel ban to Burkina Faso and Cameroon and in September he was temporarily prevented from visiting his home region. When 21 registration officials were kidnapped near Birao in the north-east in late October, the government blamed it on the CPJP and in parallel alleged that the CPJP was the armed wing of the MLPC, thus indirectly accusing its presidential candidate, Ziguélé, of being a rebel leader. This allegation was immediately rejected by both organisations. All opposition movements faced financial and organisational problems.

The CEI shortened and brought forward the period for registering *presidential candidates*. Applications by two candidates, Ziguélé and Emile Gros Raymond Nakombo (selected only weeks before as the RDC candidate), were accepted after the expiry of the official deadline. The Constitutional Court announced their acceptance, together with that of Bozizé, Patassé, Demafouth and Justin Innocent Wilité, leader of the recently created 'Congrès Centrafricain de la Renaissance', on 29 November.

On 20 April, Bozizé carried out a *government reshuffle*, leading to a further concentration of power in the hands of only a few trusted persons. He dismissed the high-profile minister in charge of communications and national dialogue, Cyriaque Gonda, and replaced him with Fidèle Gouandjika, who remained agricultural minister. Also dismissed was the minister for territorial administration and decentralisation, Elié Ouefio. His position was taken by Jules Bernard Ouandé, who combined it with being interior and security minister. Ouefio moved to the vacant position of secretary-general in the president's office – a promotion.

Foreign Affairs

UN Secretary-General Ban Ki-moon publicly expressed his concern over Charles Massi's disappearance. The drawdown of the United Nations Mission in the CAR and Chad (*MINURCAT*) had been demanded by the Chadian government without asking the consent of Bangui. MINURCAT completed its withdrawal from Birao on 15 November, handing over its two camps to the government. This left the country without a peacekeeping mission two months before scheduled national elections, but motivated an extension of the related peacebuilding mission BINUCA ('Bureau Intégré des Nations Unies pour la consolidation de la paix en Centrafrique').

Discussions were held with *Sudan* about joint border patrols. *Chad*'s army was probably involved in the recapture of Birao in late November, but relations with the northern neighbour remained problematic. Chadian herdsmen were attacked, apparently by APRD members in February and March, with the death of 18. The APRD was officially at peace with the government, which brought Bangui into a difficult situation regarding its neighbour. The bilateral commission on security matters with *Cameroon* held a meeting on 6 February. One of Bangui's concerns was the unilateral closure of a border station in Gari-Gombo since 2008. The presence of *Uganda*'s army on CAR soil was not without problems as the UFDR rebel movement saw its control over large parts of the east challenged. The Ugandan army subsequently concentrated on only few strategic positions. On 13–14 October, an AU conference attended by the defence ministers of the CAR, DRC and Uganda, as well as Sudanese representatives, was held in Bangui to discuss the management of the LRA threat. The conference recommended the formation of a joint operations centre and a joint brigade, and increased cooperation on border patrols. In late May, *US* President Obama signed the Lord's Resistance Army Disarmament and Northern Uganda Recovery Act, committing his government to develop a strategy to protect civilians in LRA affected countries – mostly the DRC, Uganda and the CAR – and also to actively contribute to ending the rebellion.

On 22 November, the trial of the DRC's former vice president Jean-Pierre Bemba for crimes against humanity and war crimes committed in the CAR started before the ICC in The Hague. From the Court's offices in Bangui (and Kinshasa), local journalists directed their questions to the parties and participants in the trial in a video conference. On 19 October, the ICC Appeals Chamber had dismissed Bemba's appeal against the decision that the case was admissible. It was expected that some key CAR actors (particularly former president Patassé) would be publicly blamed for their role in the crimes during the process.

France's Secretary of State for Cooperation Alain Joyandet visited Bangui on 8–9 April. A draft agreement on defence cooperation was signed, replacing a document dating from 1960. It was approved in December by the CAR's National Assembly.

Seven armed *Slovakians* were arrested near Nola, close to the Congo (Brazzaville) border on 1 September. Government spokesman Fidèle Gouandjika announced that a coup had been foiled. After investigations, it became clear that the men were hunters on safari. They were released on 3 September and allowed to fly home.

Socioeconomic Developments

The IMF gave moderately positive comments in its recurrent reviews of its ECF, which expired at the end of the year. An expected successor agreement had not materialised at year's end. In addition, the export sector seemed to recover, thereby reducing the foreign account deficit. The high inflationary pressures in 2008/2009 continued to recede as a result of lower spending and an increase in food crop production. Local food prices fell, leading to a drop in *inflation* to an average of 1.1%.

The IMF estimated that real GDP grew by 3.3%. The *mining sector* received new investments. The government opened an office for geological research in March, Mines Minister Sylvain Ndoutingaï created a new anti-fraud unit within his ministry, and a new minerals and gemstones auditor and a national diamond stock exchange completed the new institutional set-up aimed at attracting investors. Over the previous decade, most of the formally registered private mining firms had closed down their businesses and considerable uncertainty was also felt by the inhabitants of diamond-producing areas. With USAID support, the new Property Rights and Artisanal Diamond Development project was set up with the aim of establishing a transparent system of land ownership rights.

The most substantial investments occurred elsewhere. On 9 August, the Canada-based *gold* exploration firm Axmin was awarded a permit to start mining at its Passendro project near Bambari. Axmin had applied for the permit in March 2009 but only received it after agreeing to provide an $ 11 m signing bonus, plus three four-wheel-drive vehicles; a modest royalty of 2.25% on the proceeds of the gold sales was also part of the deal. It was speculated that the government could have earned considerably more in the long run through taxes than it acquired through the up-front payment. The contract gave Axmin a 25-year mining licence covering an area of 355 sq km.

In September, French *uranium* producer Areva launched development projects related to agriculture, access to drinking-water and basic education in the town of Bakouma to accompany the beginning of mining activities, provisionally entering a so-called test phase. The firm did not expect to reach full production until 2014–2015. Areva had reportedly acquired several blocks adjacent to its concession from Swiss-based Uranio AG, owned by Richard Ondoko, a Congolese businessman and confidant of President Bozizé.

Oil exploration was also set to begin after years of standstill caused by a long-standing dispute between a US-based oil company and the government. The International Centre for the Settlement of Investment Disputes associated with the World Bank ruled on the case. The result was a compromise favourable to the government and cleared the way to re-license the block.

On 27 July, two *Chinese* groups signed an agreement to explore for oil and gas in the north-west. On 7 August, Bozizé launched two important projects to be undertaken by an Indian company with the help of a significant *Indian government* loan of $ 29.5 m. The first was a cement factory that should help overcome the current shortage of this crucial construction commodity – cement is still imported from Cameroon at high cost. The second was a public transport project to provide 100 Indian-built buses. These new initiatives seemed to corroborate one finding in the World Bank's Doing Business Report released in November, as CAR performed reasonably well in investor protection. Overall, however, the country ranked 182 out of 183 in 2010, followed only by neighbouring Chad.

In November, the number of *IDPs* in the CAR was estimated at over 192,000 and the number of CAR *refugees* living in Cameroon and Chad at 162,000. At the same time, the country was hosting more than 31,000 refugees from the DRC and Sudan. The scale of exposure to all sorts of consequences of armed conflict was docu-mented in a report by the Human Rights Centre at the University of California (Berkeley) issued in August. Among the roughly 1,900 respondents from Bangui and four prefectures, 80% had had to flee their home at some point during the various conflicts since 2002, 21% had witnessed acts of sexual violence by armed groups, 20% had been beaten or physically attacked, and 10% had been abducted.

The 2010 *budget* approved by the National Assembly in late 2009 was fixed at CFAfr 184.6 bn on the receipt side (7.9% higher than in the preceding year) and at CFAfr 206.9 bn for expenditure, re-sulting in a deficit of CFAfr 22.3 bn, which was lower than in 2009. CFAfr 107.6 bn was to come from domestic revenues, so strong out-side support was necessary to balance the budget. It was clear that these figures would be difficult to achieve if elections were held

during 2010 as planned. As on previous occasions, election funding
had to come mostly from abroad. The EU repeatedly declared that it
would provide financial support for elections and eventually raised
its contribution to € 9.5 m.

Central African Republic in 2011

For most Central Africans this was another painful year during which they endured widespread violence. Armed clashes continued, particularly in the periphery of the country. Democratic standards declined, not least because of suspect elections for the presidency and the National Assembly. Not surprisingly, both were won by the regime in power. All available data on the social situation presented a miserable picture. President Bozizé tried to diversify his international ties, both in the sub-region and beyond.

Domestic Politics

The *presidential election*, postponed from 2010, had been set for 25 January. All the main candidates were allowed to run, although the outsider, Innocent Justin Willité, was disqualified in early January because the cheque for his registration fee bounced. Nevertheless, the opposition complained about the preparation for and conduct of the election. In fact, it was virtually impossible for the opposition to tour the country with all the restrictions on free travel that were in place. Another major problem was that the electoral register was published only one day before the poll, which made any correction impossible. This criticism culminated in the resignation of seven opposition members from the 34-strong Independent Electoral Commission ('Commission Electorale Indépendante', CEI) in protest against irregularities detected two days after the poll. The CEI, now completely controlled by the regime, announced its results on 1 February, giving incumbent President François Bozizé a two-thirds majority (66.1% of the votes), outstripping former president Ange-Félix Patassé, who ran as an independent, with 20.1%, Martin Ziguélé, candidate for the strongest opposition party 'Mouvement pour la Libération du Peuple Centrafricain' (MLPC), with 6.5%, and Emile

Gros Raymond Nakombo of the 'Rassemblement Démocratique Centrafricain' (RDC), with 4.6%. Jean-Jacques Démafouth, a former defence minister, standing as the candidate of the 'Nouvelle Alliance pour le Progrès' and not officially for his politico-military movement 'Armée Populaire pour la restauration de la République et la Démocratie' (APRD), received a mere 2.7%. On the basis of these figures, Bozizé won the election easily, but criticism continued. The four opposition candidates claimed *inter alia* that the CEI had not taken into account the votes cast at 1,262 out of the 4,612 polling stations and lodged a complaint for election-rigging against the CEI president, Joseph Binguimalé.

In the parallel *legislative elections*, the 'Kwa Na Kwa' party (KNK), supporting Bozizé, won 26 seats in the first round. Among those directly elected were the president himself, his wife Monique, his sister Joséphine Kéléfio and two of his sons. All the opposition presidential candidates also stood as candidates for the National Assembly, but had to face crushing defeats. Irregularities were potentially more important in these elections than in the presidential race. In the course of the unfolding investigations, three electoral commissioners were arrested on 9 February and the votes had to be recounted in two electoral districts. On 12 February, the Constitutional Court generally confirmed the results of the presidential election, lowering Bozizé's vote insignificantly to 64.3% (with Patassé on 21.4% and Ziguélé on 6.8%).

In light of the numerous shortcomings, as well as organisational weakness, the opposition decided on 15 February to *boycott the second round of the legislative elections*, which still took place on 27 March. The results could not but confirm Bozizé's grip on power: KNK won a total of 63 out of 105 seats in the National Assembly, but most remaining seats went to "independents" – in fact, candidates equally close to the president. The Constitutional Court subsequently annulled close to 20% of the results in both rounds of the legislative elections, a margin that did not challenge the presidential majority. Finally, by-elections were held in 14 constituencies on 4 September, again boycotted (for the most part) by the opposition. This produced the following final overall composition in the National Assembly: KNK – 62 seats; independents – 28 (most of them pro-KNK); KNK-affiliated parties – 11; MLPC – 2; RDC – 1. This represented an overwhelming majority sympathetic to Bozizé. A further by-election in Bouar was deemed necessary by a ruling of the Constitutional Court on 26 October.

The *opposition*, in particular the country's main parties, the MLPC and RDC, showed remarkable firmness in rejecting the electoral masquerade. Civilian parties, i.e. excluding the APRD, formed the 'Front d'Annulation et de Reprise des Elections de 2011' (FARE-2011), but were in fact in a weak position. The split in the MLPC, between a majority supporting former prime minister and party president Ziguélé and a minority who would still side with Patassé, was palpable and became more critical with the distance between the two candidates' election results, which humiliated Ziguélé. Both men tried to downplay the split and officially reconciled in early February. Worse was to come, when Bozizé initially refused to grant permission to Patassé to leave the country for medical treatment. When he belatedly did so, it was all too late and the former president died on 5 April at the age of 74 in Douala, Cameroon, on his way to Equatorial Guinea. The controversial and charismatic Patassé had been a major threat to Bozizé, who probably preferred being criticised for his handling of the affair to continuing to be nervous about the manoeuvres of the man he had removed by military force in 2003. But constant rumours had it that Bozizé himself was seriously ill, consulting traditional healers and visiting Nigeria in November mainly for medical treatment.

Bozizé re-appointed Prime Minister Faustin-Archange Touadéra on 22 April as the head of a *new government*. Despite the fact that the 2009 'inclusive political dialogue' had concluded with agreement that all the parties to the dialogue would be represented in future governments, this did not happen. Three members of the opposition were appointed to relatively minor positions in the government, but their parties suspended them immediately. The government of the war-torn country clearly lacked inclusiveness. Ten ministers survived the change in government, most significantly Jean-Francis Bozizé, one of the president's sons, as defence minister, and the donors' darling Sylvain Maliko as minister of planning. The controversial mines minister, Sylvain Ndoutingaï, was shifted to the finance ministry. Fidèle Gouandjika, the former minister for communication and reconciliation, lost some clout by being shifted to the agriculture portfolio and losing the prestigious title of minister of state.

The president himself seemed uninterested in the peace process and considered that the *on-going rebel activities in the periphery* hardly challenged his rule in the capital, Bangui, and the surrounding area. The army ('Forces Armées Centrafricaines', FACA) nevertheless conducted operations against the 'Convention des Patriotes pour la Justice et la Paix' (CPJP) in the north-east. Clashes between them in early February near Bria, in March near Ndélé, and again on 10 April close to Birao, resulted in government victories – at a heavy price. The clashes in Ndélé resulted in mostly civilian casualties, and 500 people were displaced, but the majority of the CPJP declared a ceasefire thereafter and officially signed a ceasefire agreement with the government on 12 June in Ndélé, followed by the dissident CPJP faction on 17 July in Nzacko. This did not amount to creating peace in the region, however, as non-government groups continued to fight each other. One confrontation involved the CPJP and the 'Union des Forces Démocratiques pour le Rassemblement' (UFDR) in the Bria area between August and October, apparently motivated by desire for control of diamond production there. Both movements were also associated with separate ethnic identities (the UFDR with the Gula, and the CPJP with the Runga). Various contradictory sources claimed that the fighting displaced between 4,500 and 15,000 people and claimed 50 lives. On 8 October, both movements signed a ceasefire agreement and left Bria. However, the CPJP still remained outside the formal Libreville Comprehensive Peace

Agreement signed by most other rebel movements in 2008. The other major confrontation took place in June around Kaga Bandoro between the APRD, mostly recruiting in Patassé's strongholds in the north, and a formerly Chadian rebel group, the 'Front Populaire pour le Redressement' (FPR). This strangely coincided with the start of a major demobilisation campaign targeting APRD fighters. On 13 June, FPR leader Babba Laddé had signed an agreement with Chadian and CAR mediators that was meant to facilitate the return of his fighters to Chad, but he later renounced the agreement and openly declared that he was pulling out of peace negotiations on 22 July. FPR fighters subsequently occupied a village between Bambari and Kouango. The overall security situation in the north, with competing rebel movements and the FACA engaging in battles that jeopardised the lives of civilians more than those of combatants, was replicated in the south-east, where combined forces fought off the formerly Ugandan-based *Lord's Resistance Army* (LRA), which staged an attack on Nzacko, far further north than its troops were believed to be. The porosity of borders was as evident as the inner weakness of the state's security forces.

In July, the minister for *disarmament*, General Yangongo, said that 1,439 rebels (out of 8,800) had been demobilised. The process was looking untransparent and disorganised when Bozizé finally took a personal interest in moving it on by mid-year. Towards year's end, new and somewhat promising figures, apparently focusing mostly on APRD combatants, were issued (4,770 men demobilised and 3,500 – mostly handmade – weapons collected). Most rebel movements expressed concern about the pace and inclusiveness of the disarmament process.

Several ministers and top officials were involved in *corruption* scandals, some of them truly embarrassing. A series of articles in 'Les Collines de l'Oubangui' pinpointed Defence Minister Jean-Francis Bozizé as being involved in the embezzlement of EU funds earmarked for a demobilised soldiers' pension fund. The editor, Faustin Bambou, was arrested without a warrant and indicted for "inciting violence and hatred", but later released by order of the court, together with another newspaper editor. Elie Ouéfio, secretary-general of both the president's office and the ruling party, lost both positions on 14 November after being accused of embezzling part of the KNK's electoral campaign budget. The general director of the 'Société Centrafricaine de Stockage des Produits Pétroliers' was arrested for embezzling close to € 3 m.

Interreligious violence erupted in Bangui on 31 May to 1 June. A mosque was burnt down by Christians, the police shot at demonstrators and a curfew was imposed. Seven deaths were officially reported.

Foreign Affairs

External reactions to the fraudulent elections were rhetorically harsh, but otherwise ineffective. On 16 May, the *EU* ambassador presented a highly critical report by international election experts to the press, using expressions such as "massive fraud" and "terrorisation of voters... by state officials and security forces". This was a significantly strong statement by the most important sponsor of the elections. Furthermore, on 27 March, EU High Commissioner Ashton criticised the on-going restrictions on freedom of movement, clearly aimed at opposition candidates. However, the EU did not threaten to cut development aid and remained one of the CAR's major donors. Paris had already urged the opposition to accept the election result on 14 February.

The *UN*'s Integrated Peacebuilding Office in the CAR (known by its French acronym as BINUCA) acquired a new leader when Ethiopian Sahle-Work Zewde was replaced by the very experienced Margaret Vogt of Nigeria. In an extended resolution on 21 December, the UNSC took positions on a number of recent urgent issues (i.e. disarmament, ceasefires, elections), but more concretely decided to extend the BINUCA mandate, on the recommendation of the UN

Secretary-General, until 31 January 2013. The UN Peacebuilding Commission held several meetings with ministers and Bozizé, but on-going violence in several parts of the country made it clear that it could hardly be considered to be in a post-conflict situation. After the closing down of the UN peacekeeping mission in November 2010, CEEAC's 'Mission de Consolidation de la Paix' (MICOPAX) moved in and, following fresh violence, opened a military base in Ndélé on 26 April.

The announcement by US President Barack Obama on 14 October that some 100 special forces troops would be sent to the sub-region to combat the LRA and train soldiers from the four affected countries (Uganda, the CAR, South Sudan and the DRC) was well received in Bangui. It was foreseen that only a small contingent of the commandos would be stationed in the CAR. Some troops arrived in December.

Bozizé fostered ties with *China*, when Vice Foreign Minister Zhai Jun was received in Bangui on 7 April. The president also made a two-day visit to *Qatar* on 21–22 November.

Only three presidents of the *sub-region* attended the re-elected president's investiture on 15 March (Idriss Déby of Chad, Ali Bongo of Gabon and Obiang Nguema of Equatorial Guinea). A trilateral meeting was held in Khartoum, Sudan, on 23 May between Déby, Bozizé and President al-Bashir of Sudan. On the agenda were issues of common security and a project to link the CAR by road to Port Sudan. Visiting Nigeria on 6–7 November, Bozizé called for stronger economic ties between the two countries and opened a consulate in Abuja. Senegal's President Abdoulaye Wade visited Bangui on 28 March.

The case against former DRC vice president Jean-Pierre Bemba for crimes against humanity committed in the CAR continued at the ICC in The Hague with the hearing of witnesses. The trial was increasingly unpleasant for the regime, as one witness, a former member of the Presidential Guard, alleged that it was the rebel army under the control of Bozizé, rather than Bemba's troops, that was raping and killing civilians in 2003. Concerns were voiced with regard to the intimidation of some prosecution witnesses whose identity had apparently been revealed, even though the chamber had put in place measures to protect their identities.

Socioeconomic Developments

According to the IMF, growth rates were expected to decline from 3.3% in 2010 to 3.1% – well below expectations. The government presented a second-generation *poverty reduction* strategy (for 2011–2015) costing $ 9.8 bn at a donor meeting in Brussels on 16–17 June and received moderate commitments. The AfDB was the most generous, promising to double its portfolio to $ 180 m and the World Bank promised a 20% increase in its allocation. An IMF delegation visited in July and the official Article IV consultations were held in November. Leaked information had it that the IMF remained critical regarding budget execution in 2010 and the resulting public debt increase. A new IMF programme was seen as crucial for initiating a new round of donor commitments more generally, as some donors had suspended their budget aid over the previous year. But controversial Finance Minister Sylvain Ndoutingaï could not attend the IMF annual meetings because of fears that he might be prosecuted in the US for charges dating back to 2005–2007, when he had ordered the Presidential Guard to attack civilians in an area controlled by the APRD.

The French *uranium* giant Areva dealt the government a heavy blow when it announced the suspension of exploitation at the Bakouma mine for one or two years. The project had given rise to high hopes for augmenting GDP growth rates and bolstering government revenues. The announcement came after the Fukushima disaster in Japan, which had a measurable impact on the price of uranium on the world market. The government thereafter threatened Areva with renegotiation of the contract, as the French firm had committed itself to launch operations in earnest by 2010.

The cumulative effect of such bad news was that observers began to fear that the debt-service ratio would rise in parallel to the government's growing inability to service its internal *debt*. In this context, the old problem of salary arrears again became a prime issue of concern. University professors went on strike, demanding their salaries, and only returned to work after lengthy negotiations on 23 September. Seven retired soldiers and gendarmes took the EU ambassador and the national mediator hostage for some hours to secure payment of 31 months of pension arrears.

On the other hand, better news came from the *mining sector* when the *Extractive Industries Transparency Initiative* granted the CAR "compliant" status. The government and operating mining companies now produced similar information on the level of taxes paid/received. The government wanted to put pressure on artisanal producers of diamonds, who would receive titles to their plots in exchange for regular information on sales and registration with the government. This was intended to end the illegal export of diamonds. Bozizé visited the oil exploration site in Boromata in the north-east in April to give a boost to further exploration activity. He announced that minimum security requirements were in place, but this was contradicted by ensuing clashes between the UFDR and the CPJP in the region. The government also hoped to increase gold production after the announcement of several successful explorations by foreign firms.

Meanwhile, the *misery* of the population continued, mostly linked to violence and inadequate public health services. In November, 'Médecins sans Frontières' published an alarming report on extremely high mortality rates in the western city of Carnot, and the UN's *Office for the Coordination of Humanitarian Affairs* put the number of IDPs at 103,000 and returnees in precarious situations at 66,500. Apart from rebel operations and the army's retaliation, local conflicts between herders and settlers were responsible for additional displacements. About 17,750 refugees from neighbouring countries were resident in the CAR. Heavy rainfall on the night of 15–16 July caused floods and significant damage in Bangui.

Central African Republic in 2012

The CAR continued on the downward spiral it had been experiencing since 1996 of frequent violent episodes with intervals too short to allow for recovery, and state capacity deteriorated further. In December, a new rebel alliance attacked major provincial cities, threatening to march on the capital, Bangui. The dreaded Lord's Resistance Army (LRA), of Ugandan origin, stepped up its activities during the year with 48 attacks recorded, despite a new multinational military initiative.

Domestic Politics

The regime showed remarkable *nervousness* on several occasions, striking out at opponents and journalists and poisoning the political atmosphere. On 16 January, the editor of the newspaper 'Le Démocrate', Ferdinand Samba, was sentenced to ten months in prison for defamation of Finance and Budget Minister Sylvain Ndoutingaï (and pardoned by President Bozizé three months later). Bozizé's nephew, Ndoutingaï, was frequently cited for involvement in corruption, as in preceding years. In an unexpected move, the president replaced him on 1 June with his predecessor (Albert Besse) without providing an explanation, but rumours circulating since May had it that it was for plotting a coup d'état. Ndoutingaï was probably one of the richest and the second most powerful individual in the country – the media had given him the title "Vice President", a non-existent position in the CAR. However, he was not only surrounded by allies but also had an impressive number of enemies (and he certainly found limited sympathy in donor circles). The influential Minister of Justice Firmin Findiro was also replaced in this context a couple of weeks later (by Jacques Mbosso).

Ndoutingaï and Findiro managed to leave the country and no investigations into their supposed crimes were initiated.

This followed on rumours of an earlier coup plot. On 6 January, four *leaders of politico-military movements* were *arrested* and accused of conspiring against national security; this was particularly noteworthy as all had roles in the disarmament, demobilisation, and reintegration (DDR) process. The most prominent of them was Jean-Jacques Démafouth, leader of the 'Armée Populaire pour la Restauration de la Démocratie' (APRD) and vice president of the DDR Steering Committee. The other three were members of the 'Union des Forces Démocratiques pour le Rassemblement' (UFDR). Both movements denied that they were involved in a conspiracy. The APRD threatened to pull out of the DDR process, but finally all detainees were freed on bail on 11 April (and the APRD announced its dissolution in May). Démafouth had been implicated in so many coup plots in the past that it was easy to accuse him of another.

The detection of *a third coup plot* was announced on 26 October. Three people were arrested, among them a former Chadian army officer – surprising given the usual high level of close cooperation between the two regimes. A military offensive in late January, jointly organised by the 'Forces Armées Centrafricaines' (FACA, the official army) and the Chadian army, destroyed the military bases of Chadian rebel leader Baba Laddé and his 'Front Populaire pour le Redressement' (FPR) in Kaga Bandoro, Kabo, Ouandago and Gondava. The FPR, variously accused of having a programme to promote the interests of Mbororo cattle herders or of simply representing highway bandits, left the area. The joint action may have been a military success but it also led to the destruction of seven villages and the displacement of more than 20,000 people. Laddé now claimed that he was aiming to overthrow the governments in both Ndjaména (Chad) and Bangui. Laddé and his troops later surrendered, and he was expelled to Chad on 3 September.

The sparsely populated eastern part of the country faced repeated incursions by rebel groups such as the *LRA*, which stepped up its activities. Forty-eight LRA attacks were recorded during the year, despite the presence of a new multinational military initiative with the help of about 100 US military advisers and involving the armies of Uganda, the DRC, the CAR and South Sudan. LRA commander Joseph Kony was believed to be in hiding in the CAR.

In December, an *alliance of rebel groups* called Séléka, the Sango word for coalition, took over most major towns in eastern and central CAR within a couple of weeks, rarely meeting any resistance. Séléka at first consisted of one wing of the 'Convention des Patriotes pour la Justice et la Paix' (CPJP), the 'Convention Patriotique pour le Salut wa Kodro', led by Dhaffane Mohamed Moussa, and the Michel Djotodia faction of the UFDR; both CPJP and UFDR had originated violent struggles in previous years and at least one faction of each had signed peace agreements with the government, in the case of the CPJP only in August (while a UFDR faction had done so in 2008). Djotodia was also only recently back from six years in exile. A CPJP splinter group emerged immediately after the agreement and attacked Sibut, Damara and Dekoa in mid-September without managing to take them. The more consequential Séléka conquest started with Ndelé (where the rebels defeated the CPJP wing allied with the government – while deployed peacekeepers did not intervene), Sam Ouandja and Ouadda on 10 December, followed by Bamingui on 15 December, Bria on 18 December and Kabo on 19 December.

The *dreaded warlord* Abdoulaye Miskine and his 'Front Démocratique du Peuple Centrafricain' now joined the rebel alliance. Thereafter, Batangafo (20 December), Bambari (23 December) and Kaga-Bandoro (25 December) were taken by the rebels, too. An effort by the FACA to retake Bambari failed on 28 December. On 29 December, the rebels took control in Sibut, only 114 miles from Bangui, and called for Bozizé's resignation. A Séléka spokesman called on the army to lay down its weapons, claiming that Bozizé no longer controlled the country. Troops in Damara, the last town on the road to Bangui under government control, were reinforced. This turn of events sent shock waves through the capital, where *self-defence committees* were formed, which checked cars and IDs of mostly Muslim nationals suspected of rebel sympathies. According to their declarations, the Séléka rebels were taking up arms because Bozizé was not honouring his commitments made at the Libreville peace talks in 2007/8. In fact, most rebel movements, including those formally at peace with the government, expressed concern about the pace and inclusiveness of the disarmament process, and this was ultimately one of the reasons given for the new upsurge of violence. There was, however, speculation about the rebels' funding and international support, since their attacks were relatively well-organised. Eric Massi, self-proclaimed spokesman of Séléka, alluded to support from circles close to Chadian President Déby, but this did not align well with Chad's official policy. Rich businessmen may also have been in a position to sponsor the rebellion.

The only major progress in the country's crucial political problems was in electoral matters. After four national workshops and consultation with civil society organisations, government and opposition agreed on a consensual text for a *revised electoral code* in early October, featuring the establishment of a permanent independent organising body, the 'Autorité Nationale des Élections', to be composed of seven members. Civilian opposition groups found it difficult – again – to get a hearing in the context of a looming new civil war. Fears that Bozizé would prepare for a change of the constitution, ultimately aiming at allowing him to stand for a further presidential term in 2016, had been a new unifying factor among *opposition parties* – and certainly added to the decline in the regime's popularity, in turn serving as a further pretext for the rebellion. At the height of the crisis, Bozizé's most visible opponent, Martin Ziguélé, leader of the 'Mouvement de Libération du Peuple Centrafricain', called for a peaceful solution.

Other events during the year reinforced the impression of a *crisis of authority.* Young men, frustrated after not being recruited into the FACA, attacked and pillaged the main prison in N'Garagba on 2 August, and over 500 detainees escaped. Compounding this problem, the prison in Sibut was looted on 15 September. Escapees remained at large, the absence of prison registers not aiding their speedy recapture. The chief of staff, General Guillaume Lapo, quickly lost the president's backing in the course of the rebel advance. Bozizé refused to receive him and appeared to favour General Jean-Pierre Dolewaye, who was in charge of military operations on the ground. At year's end, Dolewaye had suddenly disappeared.

Foreign Affairs

France was the natural ally to turn to – given the rich history of intervention by the former colonial power in Bangui. However, and in a significant move, French President François Hollande on 27 December ruled out any French intervention to save the regime, asserting those days were over. This statement followed days of protests and stone-throwing in front of the French embassy in Bangui. Bozizé nevertheless continued to call on both France and the United States to push back the rebels. Both Washington and Paris appealed to the government and the rebels to engage in dialogue. France slightly stepped up its military presence by 140 troops to an estimated force of 400. On 28 December, Washington evacuated its embassy for security reasons (and the UN ordered non-essential staff and families to leave the country).

In this situation, *Chad* was seen as the regime's major source of support. A joint commission of both countries met in N'Djaména on 29–30 October and discussed security challenges, taxation issues and the repatriation of 70,000 Central African refugees from Chad. The two countries signed agreements on customs, movement of cattle, and other matters. Chadian President Idriss Déby had indeed shown repeated interest in the stability of Chad's southern neighbour – the latest evidence was the ousting of rebel leader Baba Laddé from northern CAR (see above), and he was said to be ready to dispatch more troops to Bangui. About 20 heavily armed pick-ups were sent, officially as an interposition force, and N'Djaména also offered to host peace talks between the government and Séléka – maybe a sign that Déby was distancing himself from Bozizé. It was less clear whether all this was within the sub-regional framework of the 'Mission de Consolidation de la Paix en Centrafrique' (MICOPAX), to which Chad contributed. MICOPAX commander, General Jean-Félix Akaga of Gabon, wanted to reassure the population by stating that Bangui would be fully secured by his troops and by announcing that others would arrive to reinforce the mission. Although regional solidarity with the CAR was extraordinary at the time of MICOPAX's formation (and already during the mission that preceded it), relations with *neighbouring countries* were not free from tensions. A series of border incidents took place with Cameroon, including the arrival of a group of heavily armed poachers, who were killing elephants in a national park across the border. At the height of the rebel conquest, some neighbouring states (Cameroon, Gabon and the DRC) showed reluctance to reinforce the MICOPAX troops.

The *AU* showed above-average concern by announcing on 24 March that it would form a 5,000-strong brigade to stop Joseph Kony and his LRA. The troops would be led by Uganda but would include troops from the CAR and the DRC. The Regional Cooperation Initiative against the LRA was endorsed by the UNSC in June. Officially, the government had dispatched 350 troops in this context to the prefecture of Haut-Mbomou. The AU's monitoring structure to oversee the efforts to combat the LRA, chaired by the AU Commissioner for Peace and Security, established a Secretariat in Bangui. The Special Envoy of the Chairperson of the Commission on the issue of the LRA, Francisco Madeira, met with Bozizé and other officials on various occasions. In July, the AU launched the African Solidarity Initiative (ASI), and the CAR was one of the beneficiary countries (with Liberia, Sierra Leone, the DRC, Burundi, Côte d'Ivoire, Guinea Bissau and South Sudan). The ASI was intended to mobilise support for post-conflict reconstruction and development processes in countries emerging from crisis and conflict situations.

AU chairman Boni Yayi (Benin) travelled to Bangui on 30 December to meet with Bozizé. The meeting resulted in immediate promises by the latter to start peace negotiations in Libreville (Gabon). He also promised the formation of a government of national unity. Boni Yayi was also in contact with rebel spokespersons such as Eric Massi.

In December, *South Africa* and the CAR renewed a military co-operation agreement originally signed in 2007. Within this framework only a few dozen South African troops were deployed to the CAR, but they included a specialist VIP protection unit for Bozizé's personal security. On 31 December, South African Defence Minister Nosiviwe Mapisa Nqakula travelled to Bangui to assess the situation.

The *UN*, OIF, and AU, as well as the ambassadors of France and the US and the EU Delegation were heavily involved in breaking the deadlock between the various parties on a new electoral code. In June, the chair of the CAR section of the UN Peacebuilding Commission, Belgian diplomat Jan Grauls, resigned and had not been replaced by the end of the year. The achievements of the Peacebuilding Commission were believed to be limited so far.

Socioeconomic Developments

Following about a month's delay, the minister of finance presented his *budget* proposal for 2013 in early November. After a difficult year with little donor funding, there were high expectations of more solid planning for (and more government activity in) the upcoming year, with a total of CFAfr 261 bn in expenditure based on a projected domestic income of CFAfr 139 bn (11.8% higher than in the previous exercise) and again counting strongly on outside support. Education, health, rural development and security ranked highest on the list of ministerial portfolios that benefited. The slightly amended budget was approved by the National Assembly on 20 December with only one dissenting vote. The Economist Intelligence Unit forecast a *GDP growth* rate of 3.8% (up from 3.1% in 2011) and expected further improvements. The high deficit in the 2011 trade balance was be-lieved to have been reduced somewhat in 2012.

Given the depressing political situation, it was not surprising that the general socioeconomic position left much to be desired. As an immediate effect of the political turmoil, many people left their homes. By the middle of the year, some 65,500 people were *internal-ly displaced* (among them some 26,000 new victims seeking shelter from violence in the current year), while Chad and Cameroon were hosting another 150,000 Central Africans as *refugees*. Agricultural production certainly did not fulfil the country's potential, though the agriculture sector continued to generate more than half of GDP. WFP reported 10.2 % global acute malnutrition in children under five. *Hunger* was therefore a serious threat, and *inflation* rose to an estimated 6.8% by the end of the year; the government had followed IMF recommendations to adjust petrol prices to global standards. This created serious problems for many households. In a rare show of activity, the National Assembly demanded government explana-tions for rises in the price of basic commodities. Civil society organ-isations also pressed the government to act against price increases and received at least some response. The government tackled the *dramatic price rises* by fixing prices for a range of basic goods (in-cluding soap, sugar, vegetable oil, powdered milk, rice, flour, salt and fish) in some cities, including the capital, for six months. However, the ministerial order had barely any effect and shortages emerged in various locations. Prime Minister Faustin-Archange Touadéra con-sequently invited all major economic and business stakeholders to a meeting to discuss matters, but without tangible results.

The *IMF* argued that the failure to translate world oil prices into domestic petroleum prices in 2011 had entailed significant fis-cal losses and direct subsidies, but now had to concede the poten-tial negative impact on the most vulnerable groups of consumers. Accordingly, it advocated some mitigating social measures, includ-ing subsidising public transport. An IMF delegation visited Bangui on 9 February. On 25 June, the IMF approved a new ECF, pledging

SDR 41.8 m ($ 63.2 m) to fund reforms in public financial management. This long-awaited move was seen as a necessary catalyst for donor support more generally, and some donors agreed to renew budget support after a long wait-and-see phase. *Inter alia*, the *World Bank* approved $ 125 m in funding for transport infrastructure and regional trade, with a focus on the road link between Bangui and the port of Douala (Cameroon).

International activity was increasingly concentrated on *humanitarian aid*. After the NGO assessment that over 45,000 people were at acute risk of malnutrition in north-eastern CAR, a joint effort by humanitarian organisations made it possible to organise airdrops of food aid to seven towns in the Vakaga prefecture in August and September, reaching more than 11,000 people in need. But this was just the tip of the iceberg. The UN system's consolidated appeal process was based on the premise that 1.9 m people were in need of humanitarian assistance – almost half the country's population.

Uranium mining, once one of the greatest hopes for economic recovery, stalled. A rebel attack (attributed to the FPR) on the Bakouma site in June proved disastrous. No French nationals were hurt (although one local civilian was killed), but French mining giant Areva nevertheless declared that it would completely abandon its plans to exploit the site (after significant delays to progress in 2011).

Central African Republic in 2013

The year saw the rising and declining star of yet another politico-military entrepreneur at the helm of the state. Michel Djotodia declared himself president after a rebel alliance swept the Bozizé regime overboard. However, in the aftermath of the uprising, Djotodia was unable to stabilise his regime – and even less the country as a whole. In the western half of the country bloody encounters between predominantly Muslim Séléka groups and Christian militias spiralled out of control, leading to interreligious massacres. The humanitarian situation remained disastrous throughout the year.

Domestic Politics

The first days of the year saw new assaults by the Séléka alliance, moving closer to the capital, Bangui, and facing little resistance. A joint effort by the army, critically supported by peacekeepers of the 'Mission de Consolidation de la Paix en Centrafrique' (MICOPAX), provisionally halted the rebel advance. The MICOPAX commander issued a strong statement: a rebel advance to the strategic city of Damara would be considered a declaration of war on all Central African countries. He was confident that this warning would be heeded and, indeed, rebels and government were then prepared to send envoys to peace talks. A *peace accord* was concluded in Libreville, capital of Gabon, on 11 January, specifying that the president should remain in office until general elections in 2016. An inclusive government of national unity should be formed to serve for that period. President François Bozizé appointed the former human rights activist and opposition politician Nicolas Tiangaye as prime minister on 17 January. Tiangaye did not manage till 3 February to form a broad government of national unity; it included Michel Djotodia, leader of the 'Union des Forces Démocratiques pour le

Rassemblement', the best-known Séléka component, as vice-prime minister and defence minister, plus four other prominent rebel representatives. The Bozizé camp retained the key ministries of foreign affairs, economy, public security and mining, while civilian opposition groups and civil society were equally represented.

It was not only the Séléka combatants outside Bangui who were unhappy with this outcome of the peace process. Mohamed Moussa Daffhane, another Séléka leader and now minister of forestry, publicly declared that the rebels had not been given enough positions. Individual acts of violence perpetrated by Séléka rebels were now constantly reported. A rebel attack on Sido in the north-west by the 'Convention des Patriotes pour la Justice et la Paix' (CPJP) caused 4,000 inhabitants to flee to neighbouring Chad and was condemned by two Séléka leaders. In mid-February, probably without the consent of the ministers representing them in government, rebels attacked a number of cities, including the centrally located Sibut, and Bangassou, Gambo and Rafai in the east. Apparently anxious not to lose their power-base, five Séléka ministers (including Djotodia) began touring the interior of the country to discuss peace options and were allegedly captured by rebels on 17 March; this was a tactical ploy. A rebel commander set a 72-hour ultimatum for a number of older demands to be met (liberation of all political prisoners, departure of Ugandan and South African troops, and the dismantling of road blocks). When the three days expired, the Séléka troops attacked again and passed the strategically located city of Damara without resistance by the peacekeepers stationed there – the earlier declarations had obviously become worthless. Entering Bangui on 23 March was more difficult as South African troops put up fierce resistance, but they were soon outnumbered. Bozizé fled Bangui in the direction of Cameroon. This marked the *fourth violent regime change* in the history of independent CAR (after 1965, 1981 and 2003). Djotodia, obviously not a prisoner of the rebels, immediately declared himself president on 24 March. He dissolved the National Assembly and the Constitutional Court, suspended the Constitution and announced on 25 March that elections would take place within three years.

In search of some *minimal legitimacy*, Djotodia had himself elected as president on 13 April by a quickly formed 'Conseil National de Transition' (CNT), a provisional legislature consisting of 105 members (among them 24 representatives of political parties and 15 members of Séléka, plus representatives of all prefectures, religions, civil society organisations, etc.; it was later enlarged to 135 members). The vote took place by acclamation. Djotodia kept Tiangaye as prime minister, a further tactical step aimed at acquiring some outside recognition, but the thin veneer of constitutionality deceived nobody. Tiangaye presented a new government on 31 March; it included some names well known on the political scene plus some rebel leaders, now in more prominent positions. Djotodia changed course over time, bowing to international pressure. First, significantly, on 13 June he added two former Bozizé supporters to an enlarged government (which also included nine ministers from Séléka, seven from the former opposition parties and 16 representatives of civil society and other political parties). On 18 July, Djotodia promulgated a transitional constitutional charter, adopted on 5 July by the CNT – again, apparently under pressure. The charter fixed the transition period at 18 months and stated the ineligibility of the transitional president and the transitional prime minister to stand in future elections. On 15 August, an interim Constitutional Court was installed. The relationship between Djotodia and Tiangaye remained tense. The interim president was inaugurated on 18 August (marking the official start of the transition).

Much more dangerous for the new regime was its inability to establish order. In April, Séléka troops raided large parts of northern CAR. HRW documented the destruction of about 1,000 houses. The Séléka fighters proved undisciplined, divided not only into their five main components, but also into smaller uncontrolled units, and did not obey orders from Djotodia. The nature of Séléka as an irregular ad hoc alliance now proved to have far-reaching consequences.

In Bangui neighbourhoods, different *Séléka* units established their zones of control and started a *reign of terror*. But soon resistance grew. Serious crimes by Séléka elements, reported from all over the country, went unpunished and local self-defence groups retaliated. It was at first unclear what role the deposed president was playing in funding or arming such groups, which were summarily named *'anti-balaka'* (anti-machete). In such circumstances, it was unrealistic to believe that an orderly disarmament and demobilisation process would be possible, although some Séléka forces were officially concentrated in specific sites in preparation for such a move. Many official security forces reported back weeks or months after they had disappeared during the battle for Bangui.

Within the *Séléka leadership, major schisms* developed. Mohamed Moussa Dhaffane, senior minister of water and forests, was accused of recruiting mercenaries and buying arms; he was dismissed and arrested on 29 June. As the leader of the 'Convention des Patriotes pour le Salut du Kodro', he had headed one of the main components of the alliance that assaulted Bangui. Séléka factions had clashed with each other in the aftermath of that battle in Bangui and in Bangassou on 15 July. A further government reshuffle took place on 22 August: Nourredine Adam, one of the most prominent Séléka commanders, was replaced as minister of security and immigration by one of Bozizé's key ministers, Josué Binoua, and appointed to a secret service position. In August, more targeted attacks on the new regime were recorded, most probably master-minded by Bozizé, including attacks on villages close to Bossangoa in the west, causing 18,000 people to flee to the prefecture's capital (the number later swelled to 35,000). Many operations officially launched to disarm civilians caused serious trouble. On 28 August, one such operation in the Bangui districts of Boy Rabé and Boeing turned particularly violent. As a result, the population of those districts took refuge on the tarmac at Bangui M'Poko International Airport, bringing a halt to air traffic. On 10 September, Djotodia dismissed Chief of Staff Jean-Pierre Dollé-Waya and replaced him with the former head of the presidential guard under Ange Félix Patassé (1993–2003), Ferdinand Bombayeke. Under strong international and domestic pressure, Djotodia finally announced the dissolution of Séléka and of the CPJP as one of its components on 13 September.

However, this did not prevent the *climate of insecurity* from spreading further – with organised pro-Bozizé militias attacking Bouar in late October, and frequent attacks and acts of retaliation in Bangui, where a judge was killed on 17 November and another gravely injured shortly afterwards in a grenade attack. By that time, the on-going attacks and counter-attacks on villages and neighbourhoods were clearly following religious lines. The *interreligious violence* had spiralled out of control. Boko Haram elements from Nigeria reportedly joined Séléka fighters. However, various local roots of division were more important and were exploited. This was clear with regard to the precarious situation of minority Muslim (partly Chadian) traders in Bangui, who had already in the past made easy scapegoats in times of crisis. Previous events were also an essential element in the targeting of (Muslim) Mbororo nomads in the north-west, who had for decades been accused of being involved in highway robbery. The Catholic Sant'Egidio community invited government and religious representatives to peace talks in Rome in September and the transitional government signed the resulting "republican pact" on 7 November. The document was meant to serve as a framework to promote an inclusive national dialogue, calling *inter alia* for the disarmament of all militias, but this failed to produce tangible results on the ground. The Djotodia régime was not able to mobilise the necessary support either at home or abroad: Neither financial aid, nor the much needed military support was initially forthcoming. When French troops finally bolstered the 'Mission Internationale de Soutien à la Centrafrique' (MISCA) peacekeeping force in November, they found it more difficult than anticipated to reduce levels of violence, even in Bangui. On 5 December, anti-balaka groups launched a major attack against Muslims in the capital, killing more than 1,000 people, according to the UN, and causing the displacement of 214,000. Séléka forces were able to repel the attackers. North of Bangui, cities such as Bossangoa, Bouar, Bozoum and Paoua were the scene of continued fighting.

In these circumstances, less attention than usual was paid to the continued activities of the *Lord's Resistance Army* (LRA). However, several attacks on villages in diamond-producing areas in the east were reported in June and July, with dozens of people killed, villages burnt and about 30 people abducted (the typical LRA strategy). A hitherto unknown 'Mouvement de la Marche Populaire pour la Démocratie Centrafricaine' (MMPDC) had earlier attacked Obo in the east on 25 May. Though joint national and Ugandan forces co-operating in the framework of a Regional Task Force repelled the attack, this meant they had to redeploy to Zémio, thus making them no longer able to track LRA forces. Similarly, the little-known rebel movement 'Front pour la Restauration de l'Unité et la Démocratie en RCA' seized the diamond town of Boda in the west of the country – the movement was earlier reported to be rather active close to the Chadian border and led by the dubious businessman Sani Yalo who had been instrumental in establishing Bozizé's regime in 2003.

The CNT adopted a draft electoral code on 7 November and an 'Autorité Nationale Electorale' was appointed on 16 December to prepare for elections. However, at year's end there was *little prospect of orderly elections* being held soon. Two days later, Djotodia fired Security Minister Binoua, Finance Minister Christophe Mbrémaïdou and Rural Development Minister Joseph Bendounga, apparently without consulting the prime minister and against the stipulations of the transition arrangements.

Foreign Affairs

Peacemaking, peacekeeping and humanitarian aid were the main aspects of international involvement in the CAR. The peace agreement brokered on 11 January in Libreville by Congo's President Denis Sassou Nguesso was obviously too little, too late.

The *violent change of government* on 24 March led to immediate *international reactions*, both the UNSC and the AU issuing harsh statements. The AU suspended the CAR's membership immediately on 25 March. The AU Peace and Security Council advocated in no uncertain terms a "total isolation" of Bangui and announced sanctions including travel bans targeted at seven Séléka leaders. In accordance with Africa's inter-governmental architecture, it was, however, the CEEAC that continued to steer crisis management. Mediator Sassou Nguesso (a former coup leader) did not want to ignore the clear military victory of one party to the conflict. Djotodia ignored the travel ban and visited numerous African countries during his first months in power (Benin, Burkina Faso, Chad, Gabon, Equatorial Guinea and Sudan). However, a CEEAC summit on 3 April in N'Djamena (Chad) put pressure on the new regime. In order to normalise the institutional situation, the heads of state called for the establishment of an interim legislature in the form of the CNT. CEEAC tried to convey the impression that the Libreville peace agreement still had some validity. A follow-up committee on the Agreement met with Djotodia on 10 June and mainly discussed the political transition and the confining of Séléka fighters.

Two African countries had a particular impact on the CAR during early 2013. Some 250 *South African troops* were the only armed units putting up strong resistance to the Séléka incursion in the CAR, but they suffered heavy casualties when 13 soldiers died in the battle for Bangui (27 were wounded). News of this sent shockwaves to South Africa and also infuriated President Jacob Zuma. Zuma, accompanied by three ministers, attended the aforementioned regional summit in N'Djaména, where he agreed to the departure of the South African troops, one of Séléka's key demands. A further sub-regional summit was convened, again in N'Djamena, on 18 April, and Zuma again showed up, confirming his continued commitment. In April,

Prime Minister Tiangaye, on his first long diplomatic tour, visited not only European countries but also South Africa, in search of support.

The fact that both summits were held in *Chad* was even more significant. Chad had obviously changed sides during Bozizé's last months in power, although President Idriss Déby had originally been crucial in establishing the Bozizé regime. It was an open secret that the passivity of the Chadian peacekeeping contingent facilitated the rebel advance, the fall of Damara being clear proof of this. Unknown but substantial numbers of Séléka fighters were of Chadian origin. Chad's ambassador later denied that Chadian special forces had helped to take Bangui on 24 March, as Bozizé alleged. On 9 April, Eritrea also denied having armed the rebels, another Bozizé allegation.

At the beginning of the year, the MICOPAX *force* consisted of about 500 personnel in total, with Chad deploying some 400 and Congo, Cameroon and Gabon promising to send up to 120 each. The sub-regional organisations CEEAC and CEMAC renewed their support for the peacekeeping mission several times before the AU's Peace and Security Council decided on 19 July to authorise the deployment of an African-led mission (MISCA) for a period of six months. Its overall strength was set at 3,652, including 2,475 military personnel and 1,025 police and it was to be mainly composed of contingents currently serving in MICOPAX – the transition was initially set for August. The AU expressed the wish to see the EU and the UN assisting MISCA. The deployment of additional troops was slow, however. By 31 October, MICOPAX had deployed 2,589 uniformed personnel (mostly military, with only a few police); more than 60% were operating in the capital. An assessment of the mission by the AU and CEEAC found that many basic requirements were lacking, including maintenance and engineering capabilities, air support, command and control communication systems and ammunition. The transfer of authority from MICOPAX to MISCA was rescheduled to 19 December. A joint AU-CEEAC delegation (ministers from

Congo and Chad plus the AU commissioner for peace and security) visited Bangui on 28 December.

The bloody anti-balaka attack on Bangui and retaliation by Séléka fighters on 5 December triggered the next level of international engagement. French President Hollande had made it clear in late 2012 that France would not intervene to save Bozizé's regime from attack, but he was unable to avoid getting dragged into the crisis. On 13 October, French Foreign Minister Laurent Fabius visited Bangui and expressed France's willingness to help the country, and on 9 December Paris launched the so-called *Operation Sangaris*, deploying 1,600 troops in support of MICOPAX. Sangaris and MICOPAX started immediately by disarming Séléka fighters, some of whom were now helpless against attacks by Christian militias. The AU Peace and Security Council increased the authorised strength of MISCA to 6,000 troops on 13 December; 850 additional troops from Burundi were quickly deployed until 20 December.

The UN apparatus was again strongly involved in managing the crisis when a *UNSC* resolution on 10 October reinforced the mandate of the 'Bureau Integré de l'Organisation des Nations Unies en Centrafrique', asking for a stronger presence on the ground. On 5 December, the UNSC adopted a further resolution, not only authorising MISCA and Sangaris, but also imposing a one-year arms embargo and urging the UN secretary-general to prepare and plan the possible transformation of MISCA into a full UN peacekeeping operation. Donors tried to coordinate themselves better. A newly formed International Contact Group held a first meeting in Brazzaville (Congo) on 3 May, establishing a trust fund to support the transition, and met again in November. On the ground, the UN, AU, EU, France and the United States established a "group of five" to coordinate their actions.

The involvement of countries of the *sub-region* in the CAR crisis, and the repercussions of the crisis on the region, were a source of concern. Besides the Chadian influence, there was some speculation that South Sudan was involved (along with Séléka) in the

MMPDC, although the South Sudan authorities denied this. One of the main demands by Séléka had been the withdrawal of Ugandan troops from CAR territory. After pressure from the AU and the UN, Djotodia issued a statement on 18 June giving assurances that he would support the AU Regional Task Force set up to fight the LRA. Cameroon faced repeated cross-border incursions from armed CAR combatants.

Socioeconomic Developments

The sequence of events – with the renewed outbreak of the civil war, chaos in Bangui and the inability of the new state leadership to establish order – had widespread catastrophic consequences. Real GDP was estimated by the IMF to have contracted by about 36%. On 15 November, the transitional government provided a new revenue target of CFAfr 86 bn, only about one-third of the figure in the initial budget. Finance Minister Mbrémaïdou reported that domestic revenue would have fallen by 45% since the coup in March. The decision by the Kimberley process in mid-May to suspend diamond trading with the CAR with immediate effect was also set to have negative effects on *government revenues*, although it was clear that 'blood diamonds' did in fact help to fund the various armed groups operating in the country; the ban was meant to curtail this illegal trade. According to the IMF, the external current account deficit nearly doubled (to 10.4 % of GDP).

The decline in food production as a result of insecurity in the countryside plus supply disruptions produced important shortages, and also resulted in the acceleration of inflation from 5.9% in 2012 to an official 6.6%. The crisis in the CAR developed, in the UN terminology, into a *'complex emergency'*. UN Emergency Relief Coordinator Valerie Amos and the European Commissioner for International Cooperation, Humanitarian Aid and Crisis Response Kristalina Georgieva visited the country on 11 and 12 July. Amos declared that all 4.6 m CAR residents were affected by the conflict. About 1.6 m people were considered at that stage to be in need of assistance, including protection, food, healthcare, water and sanitation and shelter. By November, the civil war had produced 400,000 IDPs and 66,000 refugees in neighbouring countries. In November, 1.1 m people were still rated 'food insecure'. The ongoing civil war also caused widespread material damage. Looting and rape were reported from several scenes of violence, and other atrocities, including cannibalism, were reported by the international media. Establishing an exact figure for people killed proved difficult.

Women and children were strongly affected by the violence. Sexual abuse was widely reported. The Séléka alliance had many child-soldiers in their ranks (reportedly 3,500), and the anti-balaka recruited mostly children and adolescents. Many schools were attacked and looted or served as shelter. According to an international report, 70% of the schools in Bangui, 48% in Ouaka, and 44% in Ombella-Mpoko had been attacked; in some prefectures not a single school was operating. This meant that the *education* system entirely collapsed. The state-sponsored *health* system broke down entirely and only international NGOs maintained some services in some parts of the country. Of particular concern were HIV-infected people on retroviral treatment, who could no longer be treated (with a risk of further deaths and the development of resistance against some drugs). Despite increased international attention, the disaster was listed as one of the world's "forgotten crises". By mid-December, the country had received a total of $ 136 m in humanitarian assistance, representing 47% of the UN appeal launched in December 2012, with the European Commission the most important provider. The full impact of the crisis on socioeconomic development was not yet evident at year's end, but there was no doubt that recent events had taken place at enormous cost and annihilated many years of effort in several key sectors.

Central African Republic in 2014

The CAR witnessed another difficult year, starting with more armed violence throughout the country, including in the capital, Bangui. But a change in the interim leadership, massive deployment of peacekeepers and some initial negotiations between belligerents provided hope. Without the strong engagement of the international community it would have been impossible to lower tensions and mitigate the humanitarian crisis. A ceasefire agreement was signed, albeit not a full peace agreement, which seemed difficult to reach in light of the lack of cohesion of the various armed movements. The mostly Muslim Séléka alliance split into three major factions, and the Christian anti-Balaka movement was even more decentralised – local militias used the label, but would not obey orders from self-proclaimed leaders. International efforts to involve former presidents Bozizé and Djotodia in peace talks surprised the interim government in Bangui and appeared inconsistent with the sanctions regime.

Domestic Politics

The year began with a major change in *government*. In reaction to substantial international pressure, interim President Michel Djotodia, the former Séléka leader, and Prime Minister Nicolas Tiangaye resigned on 10 January. On 12 January, initial celebrations by the Christian majority in Bangui turned into mob violence targeted at mosques and shops owned by Muslims. After deliberations within the transitional parliament, the 'Conseil National de Transition' (CNT), Catherine Samba Panza, a civil society representative (and a Christian), took over as the CAR's first female (interim) president on 20 January and appointed as prime minister André Nzapayeké, who had made a career in international finance. At the time of his appointment, he was the vice president of the 'Banque de Développement des Etats d'Afrique Centrale' (BDEAC). Within his government, announced on 27 January, technocrats took most positions. Seven female ministers were among the 21 members of the cabinet. Two Séléka officials held ministerial positions and Herbert Gontran Djono Ahaba, close to Djotodia, remained minister of public works. The anti-Balaka commander Léopold Narcisse Bara became minister of youth and sports.

The *security situation* at the beginning of the year was catastrophic. In Bangui, roughly 100,000 IDPs were stranded at the airport M'poko. In Bozoum (capital of the Ouham-Pende prefecture; North-West), bloody clashes between anti-Balaka and ex-Séléka groups continued in January with heavy casualties. In Boali, 95 km north of Bangui, anti-Balaka groups targeted Muslims who were regrouping to flee to neighbouring Chad. French soldiers and a local priest intervened to stop the killings in January. Similar confrontations were recorded in Bouar, and in the villages of Bossemptele and Guen (West). In Boda (South West) and Yaloké (West) thousands of threatened Muslims had to be protected by peacekeepers. Several hundred Muslims were killed during mob violence and by organised attacks in the first three months of the year. The Séléka forces reacted and tried to regroup outside Bangui (while 2,114 were guarded by peacekeepers in preparation for their demobilisation – officially 'relocation' – in three camps in the capital). On 2 February, peacekeepers regained control over the strategically located Sibut (Kémo prefecture), where hundreds of fighters had gathered; the Séléka fighters now moved further east to Bambari. In a retaliation attack after the killing of an allied Fulani chief, Séléka fighters destroyed the village of Goussima (Centre) in May, killing 66 people and burning houses and coffee plantations. In addition, 18 people (three aid workers and 15 community leaders) died in a Séléka attack on a hospital run by 'Médecins Sans Frontières' in Boguila (North) on 26 April. Earlier, clashes had erupted in the same village when a convoy carrying peacekeepers was attacked – resulting in a temporary exodus from Boguila. Atrocities of a smaller magnitude occurred in several other places. One particularly noteworthy event was a grenade attack on 28 May on the church of Notre Dame de Fatima in Bangui, where thousands of refugees had gathered; between 15 and 20 people were killed, including the priest. The backlash against the Séléka conquest of Bangui in March 2013 was ferocious. It had been interpreted as a take-over of state affairs by the *Muslim minority* (or in some cases, strangers from neighbouring countries). Now every Muslim – whether related to the rebels or not – was seen as a target throughout the country, including in Bangui. In the spring, several convoys of trucks, protected at first by Chadian peacekeepers, carried the majority of the Muslim residents out of the city towards the Chadian border. Some smaller cities such as Bossangoa were abandoned by the Muslim community after fierce attacks by anti-Balaka forces. Pastoralists, mostly Mbororo Fulani, were associated with and had voluntarily sided with the Séléka rebels. The pattern of confrontations in the countryside was (mostly Christian) settlers, organised into militias, against cattle-herders (largely Muslim), supported by Séléka forces. Former bandits were found on both sides and specialised in cattle theft and highway robbery. Many cattle-herders had armed long before these escalations. Direct confrontations between anti-Balaka and Séléka forces were rare and concentrated in Batangafo (July/August) and Bambari. The centrally-located *Bambari* (Ouaka prefecture) first became a powder-keg when 'foreign' anti-Balaka forces (coming from Bangui) entered the city in June. Tensions grew when an internal rift between Séléka wings became very obvious. A major Séléka assembly on 9–10 May in Ndélé was attended by 1,200 participants and saw the movement's military wing renamed as the 'Forces Républicaines'. It was led by Joseph Zoundeiko, who wanted to impose his rule in Bambari, with the help of ethnic Gula fighters, while the local zone commander, Ali Darass, a former lieutenant of the famous Chadian warlord Baba Laddé, tried to hold onto his position with the help of Fulani fighters. The Séléka infighting resulted in dozens of deaths in August, with international peacekeepers unable to stop the violence. The disarmament measures used earlier had been only partially effective and the situation deteriorated: Noureddine Adam, believed to be the most powerful Séléka leader, unilaterally suspended the internal coordination mechanism and organised an assembly of Séléka leaders in Birao (6–10 July). A subsequent communiqué announced that the movement had become the 'Front Populaire pour la Renaissance de la Centrafrique', with a politbureau to be led by Djotodia. Zacharia Damane, leader of the least visible Séléka faction, the 'Rassemblement Patriotique pour le Renouveau de la Centrafrique', continued to control Bria, an important diamond-producing zone.

It became obvious that the new government was not able to stop the violence, while the international peacekeeping forces were still being built up and were not yet operating at full capacity. The need for a peace agreement was therefore strongly motivated by external actors. However, with the anti-Balaka movement being a strongly decentralised group and the *Séléka split* into three major factions (and many smaller sub-units), bringing all relevant actors to the negotiating table became a huge challenge. At the end of a tumultuous peace forum in Brazzaville (Congo), a *ceasefire agreement* was signed on 23 July. The Séléka faction led by Moussa Dhaffane took part in the meeting, but the potentially strongest faction, led by Noureddine Adam, who was under international sanctions and in hiding in Birao to avoid arrest, did not attend. Noureddine (first vice president) later unilaterally deposed Dhaffane (second vice president) and also fell out with Zoundeiko. Further meetings of various factions confirmed the deep split, and Darass created his own 'Unité pour la Centrafrique' on 25 October. Patrice Edouard Ngaissona, a minister under former president Bozizé and increasingly seen as the most powerful spokesperson for the *anti-Balaka* movement, signed the ceasefire agreement on their behalf. It is important to note that Ngaissona was believed to be directly implicated in attacks against MISCA ('Mission Internationale de Soutien à la Centrafrique sous

Conduite Africaine') peacekeepers in March. He faced strong competition from other ambitious individuals within this extremely heterogeneous movement. Leaders of two smaller rebel movements also signed the text.

Following the Brazzaville ceasefire agreement, the Nzapayeké government resigned on 5 August and, on 10 August, Samba-Panza chose a *new prime minister*: Mahamat Kamoun, a Muslim and former close associate of Djotodia. Many Séléka leaders rejected Kamoun as they had not been consulted before his appointment. It was obvious that the Séléka leaders expected some sort of compensation for their loss of power only a few months after their conquest of Bangui. On 22 August, Kamoun formed a government that gave the armed movements more symbolic representation. In fact, three Séléka members became ministers (for transport, telecommunications and cattle-breeding). The anti-Balaka movement was given two positions (environment and tourism). Armel Ningatoloum Sayo, the leader of the small rebel movement, 'Révolution et Justice', operating mostly around Paoua, became minister of sports and youth. Armed movements were therefore well represented in the interim government. Twelve members of the former government remained in the new team, but five of them changed posts (including the former interior minister, Aristide Sokambi, now minister of defence); the government grew to 31 members.

A new round of *confrontations in Bangui* erupted in October, when anti-Balaka groups erected barricades in response to murders allegedly committed by Séléka elements. This led to violence that cost dozens of lives and 6,500 civilians were forced to abandon their homes. In Zémio, intercommunity violence in November resulted in the exodus of 80% of the population, and 20,000 inhabitants of Kouango crossed the Oubangui River when new confrontations between anti-Balaka forces and Fulani cattle herders erupted in December.

As progress on the preparations for a constitutional referendum and elections was slow, the *transition calendar* had to be revised several times. Elections were now scheduled for the summer of 2015 (instead of February). The transition had originally been set to last not more than 18 months with an option to extend the process by a further six months, but it was only on 24 June that the president signed a decree on the organisation and functioning of the National Electoral Authority. The transitional government and the CNT struggled to deliver tangible public benefits and clearly lacked legitimacy. Some parties were already prepared for elections; they included the 'Mouvement de Libération du Peuple Centrafricain', which selected former prime minister Martin Ziguélé as its candidate on 22 November. On 22 December, the CEEAC mediator, Congolese President Sassou Nguesso, after receiving the green light from the UNSC, agreed to extend the transition period and four days later Prime Minister Kamoun announced a new transition calendar with a constitutional referendum planned for May and legislative and presidential elections scheduled for July and August 2015. The CNT adopted an amended electoral law on 27 December, but it had not been promulgated by the end of the year. A local consultation process on the constitution and the envisaged peace order started in December (ahead of a national forum) with government ministers deployed to the provinces.

A number of additional conflict risks were far from eliminated. The Lord's Resistance Army (LRA) in the south-east of the country had not yet surrendered. On 29 June, an attack on the Ugandan army stationed in Bakouma that was attributed to the LRA allied to some Séléka splinter groups resulted in three dead. Cross-border raids by smaller rebel movements active in Chad and the CAR, or Cameroon and Chad, were still able to trigger violence as was the involvement of the official security forces of both countries.

The planned *redeployment of the state administration* throughout the country proved very difficult. Some of the prefects installed in the provincial headquarters with the help of international peacekeepers immediately boarded a plane back to Bangui after the official ceremonies. Séléka forces even prevented the installation of a new prefect in Ndélé. The limitations of the state administration became clear when a joint CAR and Sudanese army contingent had to leave Birao in response to an ultimatum set by Noureddine on 26 June. In both Birao and Ndélé, the establishment of prefects ultimately failed (formally 50 out of 71 sub-prefects were reinstalled). At one point, a document leaked to the press indicated that some Séléka leaders were considering splitting of the country in two.

Foreign Affairs

Pressure on the UNSC to act on the CAR crisis grew constantly. The AU-led MISCA peacekeeping mission, mandated and established in December 2013, was perceived as not well-enough equipped and staffed (starting with 4,500 soldiers and intended to grow to 6,000). Burundi and Chad (850 soldiers each) provided the largest contingents. The mission was mainly funded by the EU with € 125 m from its African Peace Facility, covering allowances, accommodation and food. It was clear to most New York-based diplomats that MISCA should only be a temporary arrangement until a UN mission became operational. In early March, UN Secretary-General Ban Ki-moon recommended a 12,000-strong UN peacekeeping operation and MISCA peacekeepers in Bangui came under fire from anti-Balaka groups several times during the same month. With Resolution 2149, passed on 10 April, the UNSC finally approved the 'Mission Multidimensionnelle Intégrée des Nations Unies pour la Stabilisation en République Centrafricaine' (MINUSCA), to be formed of 10,000 military and 1,820 police personnel. MINUSCA finally took over from MISCA on 15 September and had at that time 7,500 operatives. In the meantime, an EU-sponsored mission was also in the making. On 20 January, EU foreign ministers agreed to launch the ninth EU military operation, and quickly received a UNSC mandate (on 28 January). In mid-April, the EU Force (EUFOR) mission became operational, reaching full operational capability on 15 June with 700 troops. France contributed by far the largest contingent (and the force commander). Other EU members (Spain, Finland, Georgia, Germany, Italy, Latvia, Luxembourg, Netherlands, Poland and Romania) contributed smaller contingents. The EUFOR mission was mostly assigned to provide security at Bangui airport and in two districts of Bangui, thus making it possible for MISCA (later MINUSCA) and the French Operation Sangaris to reach out to the hinterland. On 20 October, the UNSC extended the EUFOR mandate for a further six months until 15 March 2015. The European Commission and individual EU member states scaled up their humanitarian aid from € 20 m (in 2012) to € 128 m.

France was now more involved militarily than it had been since downsizing its presence in the late 1990s. Its Operation Sangaris was crucial for security in Bangui, and France also contributed troops to MINUSCA and EUFOR. On 4 January, the French government reported that the situation had calmed. Gradually, containment activities spread from the capital to the hinterland, starting with the control of the Bangui-Bossangoa axis and the road link to Cameroon. On 25 February, after a visit by French Defence Minister Jean-Yves Le Drian, the French National Assembly approved the expansion of Operation Sangaris by 400 to 2,000 men (including 50 policemen). France's involvement proved effective in the western part of the country. Sangaris commander Francisco Soriano also engaged in diplomacy by meeting religious and civilian authorities; he was dismissed in June, when French media reported that the operation was collaborating closely with some anti-Balaka units. By the end of the year, Sangaris had lost two soldiers, and 120 had been injured since the start of the operation a year before. In December, the French government announced its intention to reduce Sangaris to 1,500 soldiers, as the security situation had improved (despite a surge in criminal activities); this clearly did not reflect the on-going insecurity in the centre of the country and the very limited control exercised by peacekeepers over the east.

The immediate precursor of Djotodia's resignation was a special *CEEAC* summit convened by President Idriss Déby of Chad on 9–10 January. The entire CNT was invited to the Chadian capital, N'Djamena. Djotodia decided to step down at the end of the summit. *Chad's* involvement in both the civil war (first on Bozizé's side, and then in support of Séléka) and peacekeeping efforts remained highly controversial. A Chadian MISCA company was attacked upon arrival in Bangui on 28 March and the Chadians allegedly indiscriminately shot at civilians in retaliation, creating even more unrest. In response, on 3 April, Chadian President Déby decided to withdraw the Chadian contingent from MISCA without prior consultation. While mostly welcomed on the ground, this created logistical problems and further unease. The Chadian contingent was one of the strongest numerically and was responsible for security in Bossangoa. With the departure of the Chadians, 540 Muslims under their protection had to leave with them for Chad. Armed incursions from Chad into northern CAR, most probably with consent, if not orders, from N'Djamena, continued and the border was officially closed on 4 May. In one instance, the sub-prefect of Markounda was arrested and taken to the Chadian capital for interrogation.

Cameroon felt the effects of the on-going crisis as armed groups from the CAR entered Cameroonian territory in September and October, leading to a temporary closure of the border. The 'Front Democratique du Peuple Centrafricain' was probably the initiator of some of these actions, as their leader, Abdoulaye Miskine, had been held in Cameroon since 2013. After mediation by Sassou Nguesso, Miskine was released on 27 November in exchange for 26 abducted hostages, including a Polish priest. The *Ugandan army* clashed with Séléka troops at the end of June, killing 15 fighters; a spokesman for the Ugandan Army stated that Séléka had forced civilians to give food and medicine to the LRA and that they were also jointly engaged in trade in ivory and minerals. This escalation meant that it would be difficult for Ugandan soldiers to join UN peacekeeping forces, as Kampala had wished.

A *UN panel of experts* continued to work on the CAR situation. In their final report, they attributed killings of civilians, including humanitarian aid workers, in the period 5 December 2013–14 August 2014 to Séléka (617) and anti-Balaka (861), with total casualties estimated at 3,000. The experts also looked into the illicit trade in and exploitation of natural resources (gold, diamonds and timber) and reported on the use of forced labour in gold mines involving Séléka commanders in their strongholds; in addition, individual Séléka commanders were engaged in diamond smuggling. Anti-Balaka members were doing the same in the western part of the country. A debate (mostly carried on outside the country) as to whether the targeting of the Muslim minority would meet the *criteria for genocide* played a part in attracting attention to a forgotten crisis. However, some direct implications of this quarrel were also felt on the ground. In December 2013, the UNSC had established an *investigation commission* into human rights violations, led by the highly respected Cameroonian lawyer Bernard Muna, formerly the deputy prosecutor at the International Criminal Tribunal for Rwanda. The commission was only able to start investigations in April because of the highly hostile environment. Its first provisional report was issued in July and stated: "The fact that there is an anti-Muslim propaganda from certain non-Muslim quarters does not mean that genocide is being planned or that there is any conspiracy to commit genocide or even a specific intent to commit genocide." This was not well received by international human rights NGOs. The final report followed the same line and was issued on 19 December. It argued that government forces under Bozizé, as well as the Séléka and the anti-Balaka groups, had been involved in serious violations of international humanitarian law and gross abuses of human rights. The commission could not establish genocidal intent by any party to the conflict but stated that this did not diminish the seriousness of crimes committed or give any reason to assume that in the risk of future genocide had subsided. A pattern of ethnic cleansing had been executed by the anti-Balaka in the areas in which Muslims had been living, amounting to a crime against humanity. Not unrelated to such investigations were strong actions: on 9 May the UNSC Committee decided to impose targeted *sanctions* on François Bozizé, the anti-Balaka leader (and close aid of Bozizé), Lévy Yakité, who had been involved in numerous atrocities, and Noureddine Adam. US President Barack Obama extended the sanctions to Michel Djotodia and warlord Abdoulaye Miskine. Yakité later died in a road accident in France. The French government froze the French assets of Jean-Francis Bozizé, son of the former president, when suspicions arose that he was planning a coup d'état in November. In a resolution on 18 December, the UNSC threatened to extend sanctions to other individuals. On 24 September, the ICC formally opened an investigation into crimes committed since 2012. While many observers welcomed this initiative, its short-term effect was questionable, given that the ICC had not ended proceedings in the case of Jean-Pierre Bemba, who was awaiting judgement for crimes committed in the CAR back in 2001. In December, much to the surprise of the government, mediator Sassou Nguesso together with the Kenyan government initiated *parallel peace talks* in Nairobi (Kenya) involving Djotodia and Bozizé.

Socioeconomic Developments

The misery of the population continued as a result of the dire security situation. Towards the end of the year, UNHCR reported that there were about 410,000 IDPs and 420,000 refugees – nearly a fifth of the population and four times as many as after the last round of hostilities (2008). According to the UN Office for the Coordination of Humanitarian Affairs (OCHA), 2.7 m Central Africans (out of a total population of 4.6 m) were *in need of assistance* at the end of the year. Apart from security, the establishment of a minimum level of material well-being was also a target of the international community. As of 31 December, donors had committed $ 376.4 m (68%) of the $ 555 m requested within the CAR Strategic Response

Plan. OCHA noted that early recovery, education and emergency shelter would be the least funded sectors. The peacekeeping missions concentrated part of their efforts on keeping the Bangui-Douala corridor open to allow *humanitarian aid* to come through. State revenues were very limited and mostly used to pay the security forces, while the World Bank ensured the payment of civil service salaries. The IMF approved financial assistance worth close to $ 13 m under a Rapid Credit Facility to support emergency recovery programmes. The IMF took a critical look at the *economic prospects* and projected that the scarcity of basic consumer goods would translate into a steady rise in prices, leading to an inflation rate of 11.6% at the end of the year (according to UN figures even 15.3%) – well above the convergence criterion adopted by CEMAC. Most of the population lacked access to food. The local *cattle market* was completely distorted, with anti-Balaka groups stealing cattle from Fulani nomads, and selling meat in the larger cities at lower prices. Some Fulani had to leave their cattle behind when they fled the country. Prospects for stabilising that market were grim. Agricultural projects funded by international partners benefitted only 110,000 households.

The state finances were in a difficult situation. Internal revenue receipts totalled $ 92 m (against a projected $ 103 m). The entrenched *war economy* structures were partly responsible: the CAR had been temporarily suspended from the Kimberley Process Certification Scheme in May 2013, resulting in a ban on official diamond exports. This had immediate effects. While the accredited merchants in Bangui continued to purchase diamonds, *diamond smuggling* – probably via neighbouring states (Cameroon and Sudan) – rose to an estimated additional 140,000 carats (worth $ 24 m). Some were seized in Belgium. The UN panel of experts suggested their origins lay in Sam-Ouandja and Bria, a zone under Séléka control. Diamond zones in the west, such as Boda, were in the hands of anti-Balaka groups. Séléka commander Ali Darass was reportedly able to build up a parallel taxation system in his stronghold of Bambari and its surroundings. The UN panel of experts estimated that he would be able to raise $ 150,000 per year in taxes from local gold production, and a similar amount from the coffee trade (from Bambari to Sudan).

Central African Republic in 2015

This was a year of progress towards the end of a prolonged transition from civil unrest to democratic rule and limited stability, despite the general precariousness of all achievements. A peace forum and the referendum on a new constitution prepared the ground for holding the first round of presidential and legislative elections shortly before the end of the year. However, renewed hostilities in the centre of the country around Bambari and Kaga-Bandoro and above all a number of serious confrontations in the capital Bangui reminded both the population and the international community that the overall situation remained volatile.

Domestic Politics

On 7 January, interim President Catherine Samba Panza nominated the 22 members of the Preparatory Commission for the Bangui Forum, an elite gathering designed to create reconciliation and set the stage for the *final period of the transition to constitutional rule*. Local consultations in preparation for the Forum were launched by this commission at the end of January; they met with organisational difficulties (reportedly just 4,000 people took part in some selected cities outside the capital) and with outright scepticism, especially in areas controlled by the Muslim-based Séléka alliance. About 400 Muslim demonstrators took to the streets of Bangui on 23 January to protest against their perceived under-representation in that process. Facilitators of the consultations on 11 March held their final workshop and produced a synopsis of the fears and desires of the population. On 27 February, four former prime ministers, the vice president of the transitional parliament ('Conseil National de Transition', CNT) and the president of the Bangui Forum preparatory committee, plus some political heavyweights, signed an appeal for national reconciliation at the Rome headquarters of the Community of Sant'Egidio, a well-known peace-making organisation supported by the Catholic Church. The *Bangui Forum* was eventually able to take place on 4–11 May, with 600 participants representing the transitional government, rebel groups, civil society, religious groups and the prefectures, as well as refugees and neighbouring countries. It produced a list of recommendations, *inter alia* to postpone elections from July to later in the year (and therefore to push back the end of the entire transition) as well as the introduction of a truth, justice and reconciliation commission (building on the work of local peace committees). At the margins of the Forum, an accord was signed on 5 May between the government and representatives of ten armed movements to stop the recruitment of children, the so-called 'Pacte Républicain' was agreed, which – amongst more vague principles – called for the installation of a Special Criminal Court, and a DDR and repatriation agreement was signed on 10 May. The Séléka wing under Ali Darassa released about 400 child-soldiers from its ranks on 14 May as one tangible consequence of the Forum's appeal. The creation of the Special Court, already discussed within the CNT before the Forum, was imminent after the promulgation of the relevant legislation on 3 June, but it was unclear who would provide the funding for this form of transitional justice.

The *transitional bodies* enjoyed little popular support and complaints about corruption were frequently voiced. Interim President Samba-Panza made adjustments to her *government* three times over the year. On 16 January, she changed the positions of four ministers: four new faces entered and four left the government. Most significant was the promotion of Marie Noëlle Koyara from minister of rural development to the position of defence minister, the first time since independence that a woman held this position. The next reshuffle, on 21 July, saw the arrival of Sébastien Wénézoui, one of the prominent anti-Balaka leaders, and of a new foreign minister. On 29 October, Samba-Panza again slightly restructured the transitional government and made only a few new appointments, the most notable being the removal of the two ministers responsible for security issues – after the serious wave of violence that hit Bangui – including Koyara, who was replaced by the well-known judge Joseph Bindoumi. Mahamat Kamoun remained prime minister throughout. The former Séléka alliance continued to provide three minor ministers (who were, however, officially banned from their organisations), while anti-Balaka groupings felt underrepresented with only Sébastien Wénézoui as environment minister.

The political-military movements appeared to be weakened by ever-growing *fragmentation*. In the anti-Balaka camp, Wénézoui started a reconciliation campaign with Muslims and created his own party, as did his most visible rival, Patrice Edouard Ngaïssona. Within the former Séléka alliance, Nourredine Adam, leader of the potentially biggest faction, the 'Front Populaire pour la Renaissance de Centrafrique' (FPRC), took the most uncompromising stance, *inter alia* by appealing for a boycott of the 13 December referendum, and one day later declaring an autonomous 'Republic of Logone' in the north-eastern part of the country (with Kaga-Bandoro as its provisional capital). In contrast, Ali Darassa, heading the second most important party, the 'Union pour la Paix en Centrafrique' (UPC), invited his followers to vote in the referendum. In the end, 93% of those who voted (with a 38% turnout) voted in favour of a text that had not circulated widely, and consequently was never publicly discussed. In a country plagued by violent political overthrows the most important innovation of the *new Constitution* was potentially the exclusion of all coup, mutiny or rebel leaders from political office (Art. 28) plus the creation of a senate as a chamber to represent the 'territorial collectivities' (i.e. above all the prefectures; Art. 73).

The *security situation* remained a source of serious concern, with various local constellations producing different forms of confrontation. After the arrest of Chadian warlord Baba Laddé on CAR territory in late 2014, UN peacekeepers of the 'Mission Multidimensionnelle Intégrée des Nations Unies pour la Stabilisation en République Centrafricaine' (MINUSCA) quickly deported this embarrassing prisoner on 2 January to Chad, where he was immediately jailed. The overall stability did not improve, however. The MINUSCA mission even had to learn that it could itself trigger escalation, when it arrested the anti-Balaka leader Rodrigue Nagibona (aka Andilo) on 17 January. Andilo followers kidnapped a French humanitarian worker two days later (she was released on 23 January) and Minister of Youth and Sport Armel Sayo, himself the leader of an armed movement ('Révolution et Justice') on 25 January (he was released on 10 February). This made it clear that MINUSCA was not even able to protect government officials. Even more embarrassing for MINUSCA was that, on 28 September, 677 detainees (about one-third of whom were anti-Balaka elements) managed to escape from the Ngaragba prison in Bangui. Sexual misconduct on the part of some MINUSCA personnel also undermined the acceptance of the mission.

The *Christian-Muslim divide* continued to be salient, at times translating into direct confrontations between ex-Séléka forces claiming to protect Muslim minorities and anti-Balaka groups claiming to represent local or Christian majorities and/or involving peacekeepers, but such conflicts were only superficially religious in content. In Mambere Kadei prefecture, a series of confrontations between Fulani herders from Cameroon and anti-Balaka groups led to the killing of 40 civilians on 2 May. Clashes between Mbororo herders and the local population in mid-May caused the death of nine civilians and the displacement of more than 1,460 people from surrounding villages to Kaga Bandoro. The main religious leaders, Archbishop Dieudonné Nzapalainga (Catholic Church), Imam Kobine Layama (Muslim community) and the Reverend Nicolas Guerekoyame-Gbangou (Evangelical churches) constantly called for moderation and were most clearly the opinion-leaders with a peace agenda. They were highly praised outside the country, but could not prevent all ethno-religious confrontations on the ground. After a fatal attack on a Muslim taxi-driver in Bangui at the end of September, severe communal clashes erupted in in the city, which led to 77 people being killed and 400 injured; in addition, about

30,000 were forced to flee their homes and entire neighbourhoods were burnt to ashes. Guerekoyame-Gbangou narrowly escaped when angry Muslim youths searched for him in a retaliatory move on 26 September; two Catholic churches were destroyed. This did not prevent *Pope Francis* travelling to the CAR on 29 November with his anticipated message of peace and tolerance; his schedule included a visit to a mosque under siege by Christian militias in Bangui. The Pope's visit was greeted from all sides as sending an important signal for a possible return to coexistence.

In the previous month, on 26 August, clashes had erupted between militias in Bambari, causing thousands to flee their homes. Ethnic or religious motives were certainly at work, but all the armed factions were more visibly in pursuit of *material aims*, e.g. of controlling mining sites and trade roads. In fact, extensive areas of the country, particularly the border zones to the east and the north, were not under government control. Infighting within the former Séléka alliance sometimes ended in bloodshed. Smaller groups also continued to be a threat more locally. According to a detailed account by Dominic Ongwen, a commander of the Lord's Resistance Army, who was captured by a Séléka group and handed over to US forces in January, the size of this movement had dramatically shrunk to only 38 fighters in the CAR. In the western and northern border zones with Chad and Cameroon, anti-Balaka groups and the armed movements 'Front Démocratique du Peuple Centrafricain' (FDPC) and 'Révolution et Justice' challenged state authority, although the latter was represented by its leader within government. MINUSCA tried to secure main road corridors, but also robustly combated the FDPC, although FDPC leader Abdoulaye Miskine, who had boycotted the Bangui Forum, stated that his movement was not creating instability as the UN claimed, and pointed instead to Boko Haram elements infiltrating from Cameroon. At year's end, some 450,000 *refugees* plus 450,000 *IDPs* (together roughly 20% of the population of 4.8 m) were waiting for conditions to improve to allow their return.

Arranging for refugees and IDPs to vote was one of the organisational challenges in the preparation for the elections, but the plans seem to have worked at least for refugees in Cameroon and Congo. Building on the experience of the referendum the transitional authorities, particularly the 'Autorité Nationale des Elections' (ANE), felt confident enough to hold the *first round of both legislative and presidential elections* on 30 December, three days later than planned according to the repeatedly adjusted timetable. As in every previous smooth election in the CAR (1993, 1998, 1999), the logistics relied heavily on military transport provided by external troops. On 8 December, the Constitutional Court excluded ten declared candidates from the contest, most importantly the anti-Balaka leader Patrice-Edouard Ngaissona (for his numerous infractions to the law) and former president François Bozizé (because he was not resident in the CAR). It was clear that strong international pressure was exerted to exclude Bozizé (who was under UN sanctions), but this was not mentioned in the court ruling. The decision, immediately condemned by Bozizé, triggered violence in Bangui; five people were killed in the PK5 district and confrontations also occurred on the same day in Batangafo. Thirty candidates were allowed to stand, including sons of former presidents (Patassé, Kolingba), former prime ministers (Dologuélé, Touadéra, Ziguélé) and former ministers. Their chances were largely unclear, given that free elections had not been held since 1999 – Bozizé had strongly manipulated elections under his rule. The ANE did not announce the election results until early January 2016.

Foreign Affairs

The CAR remained a constant item on the agenda of the *UNSC*. MINUSCA, established in April 2014, became fully operational in spring. On 28 April, the UNSC passed a resolution to renew the MINUSCA mandate and authorised a slightly increased limit of

10,750 military personnel, including 480 military observers and staff officers and 2,080 police personnel. The deployment figures remained below that maximum until the end of the year. Within MINUSCA, the 1,552 international police personnel were particularly important for security. At year's end, some 9,110 blue-helmets provided substantial security coverage but without being able to fully control the vast territory. On 17 November, in preparation for the election phase, the UN Secretary-General asked for and received from the UNSC a temporary deployment of 300 personnel from the quick reaction force in Côte d'Ivoire under an inter-mission cooperation arrangement. On 17 December, the UNSC decided to add Haroun Gaye (FPRC leader in Bangui) and Eugène Ngaïkosset (aka 'the butcher of Paoua') to its sanctions list for incitement to violence in the preparatory phase of the elections. African governments (particularly Chad and Kenya) had not applied the travel ban against Bozizé and Adam, raising doubts as to the effectiveness of the sanctions regime.

The EU-sponsored mission of 700 soldiers focusing on Bangui ceased in March in line with its mandate; a small military advisory mission remained on the ground, however, in order to promote security sector reform. Additionally, after a reduction in the size of the force in April, France still had some 1,500 to 1,700 of its *Sangaris* mission troops on the ground – and it was also contributing soldiers to the MINUSCA and EUFOR RCA (EU Force in the CAR) missions. It was clearly the most important security actor in the country.

The MINUSCA mission faced several crises in which it had to deploy force – and took a few *casualties*. On 10 April, a reported 300–400 partially armed demonstrators attacked the MINUSCA camp in Kaga Bandoro, wounding 10 peacekeepers. Around Mbres, MINUSCA and French forces engaged in robust actions to stop conflicts between Fulani and ex-Séléka on the one hand and anti-Balaka troops on the other. MINUSCA also investigated attacks like one in Kouango at the end of April, confirming that 36 abandoned villages were found, including 27 that had been totally or partially burned down. The UNSC condemned in the strongest terms an attack on a MINUSCA convoy travelling from Damara to Ngerengou, during which one peacekeeper from Burundi was killed and another injured. Similarly, it expressed shock at an attack on a MINUSCA checkpoint in the divided town of Batangafo, which followed an outbreak of violence in the local IDP camp. One peacekeeper from Cameroon was killed in the incident.

CEEAC also devoted much energy to the CAR crisis. Meeting in N'Djamena (Chad) on 25 May, the Conference of Heads of State and Government authorised a 'technical' extension of the transition to 31 December in order to permit the transitional authorities to organise the elections appropriately. An extraordinary summit in Libreville (Gabon) on 25 November focused on the upcoming elections in the CAR. Mediator Sassou Nguesso (Congo) was not the best-loved man in Bangui as he had in late 2014 initiated *parallel peace talks* in Nairobi (Kenya) with former presidents Djotodia and Bozizé, both under UN sanctions, in clear contradiction of the Bangui Forum idea and drawing on the support of the Kenyan government. The transitional government rejected the separate peace process on 25 January, not least because it was itself not represented in Nairobi. On 14 April, Bozizé and Djotodia signed a 'Nairobi declaration' in the presence of Kenyan President Uhuru Kenyatta and Vice President William Ruto, who were both under indictment at the ICC. Observers quickly termed the deal meaningless. The Cessation of Hostilities Agreement, signed on 23 July 2014 in Brazzaville, had provided for an implementation mechanism, including a Follow-up Commission and a Technical Committee. The UN Secretary-General noted that these did not adequately monitor or prevent the frequent violations of the agreement, thereby indirectly also criticising Sassou Nguesso. Djotodia (for Séléka) and one anti-Balaka leader had signed the Cessation of Hostilities Agreement on 8 April, prior to the Nairobi declaration.

The *AU* also paid close attention to events in the CAR and hosted several meetings of the International Contact Group for the CAR under the co-chairmanship of Peace and Security Commissioner Smail Chergui and Congolese Defence Minister Richard Mondjo. The AU Commission convened a DDR Sensitisation at the AU headquarters on 25–26 November

On 21 December, the *UN Panel of Experts* issued a substantial report on the war economy that had taken root and on infractions of the sanctions regime, pointing at sub-regional involvements and repercussions. *Cameroon*, temporary home to close to 250,000 refugees from the CAR, remained particularly exposed to the crisis. On 8 January, Cameroonian authorities arrested an arms dealer in Kenzou. A sizable proportion of smuggled CAR diamonds reportedly went through Cameroon, contributing to the a growing criminalisation of the economy. Truck drivers in Garoua-Boulai on the Cameroonian side of the border took strike action (in June, August and October) in protest against the inability or unwillingness of both MINUSCA and the official armed forces to protect them from attacks by the FDPC and unidentified gangs.

The *Sudanese* authorities were believed to at least tolerate illegal trade in coffee and sugar from Séléka-occupied territory in the CAR. Séléka fighters and commanders could travel to both Chad and Sudan without any hindrance, and Nourredine Adam in particular maintained his networks in the neighbouring country. However, there was *fierce competition between the three main Séléka factions* over the lucrative control of trade routes to Sudan. Sudanese arms traders dominated the market in the eastern part of the CAR. According to the UN Panel of Experts, *Chadian* security and military personnel were constantly committing human rights violations against CAR nationals, including killings, looting and destruction, forced displacement, extortion, illegal detention and violation of the right of return of CAR refugees in Chad), an allegation rejected by N'Djamena. Although officially closed, the common border could be passed unilaterally by Chadian traders pursuing business in the

CAR, but not by ordinary CAR nationals. Chadian security forces mobile checkpoints were present as far as 25 km inside the CAR. Chad and the *DRC* each hosted more than 90,000 CAR refugees.

Socioeconomic Development

After a dramatic fall of 36% in its *GDP* in 2013 and a mere 1% growth in 2014, the Economist Intelligence Unit estimated the CAR's economic growth at 3.3% for 2015. Some sectors were slowly recovering, most notably agriculture and trade, but the formal CAR economy remained in limbo. Humanitarian aid had replaced market relations in large parts of the country, while armed movements controlled most of the illegal trade in diamonds, gold, cattle and other products. In the south-west, some anti-Balaka leaders even managed to obtain official mining licences.

With high demands on every side, e.g. for the restructuring of the security sector, the government, with its limited means, was barely able to make an impact. An increase in expenditure meant that the *public finances* fell back into a deficit, which the Economist Intelligence Unit estimated at 5.1% of GDP. The IMF disbursed $ 7.9 m in March and $ 11.8 m in October within its Rapid Credit Facility. After the conclusion of the Bangui Forum, the EU committed itself to additional funding from a development trust ('Fonds Bêkou'; with contributions from France, Germany and the Netherlands) including € 40 m of critically needed budgetary support.

The UN Panel of Experts provided detailed information on the *illegal trade routes* of conflict minerals out of the CAR in which armed movements or individuals were involved. The picture painted was one of widespread plunder. The government saw as one of its crucial aims the reestablishment of orderly practice in the diamond trade. In fact, the country remained suspended from the Kimberley Process Certification Scheme, which translated into a ban on official diamond exports. By an administrative decision, this ban was partially lifted in August for production zones under government control (i.e. in the west), if transparency prevailed and on condition that safeguard conditions would be met. It was also hoped that this decision would facilitate the export of stocks (60,000 carats with an estimated value of $ 7 m) accumulated since early 2014. It also meant that all diamond production in the east and the centre would still fall under the sanctions; there were few signs that this could change in the immediate future.

According to the UN Office for the Coordination of Humanitarian Affairs (OCHA), 2.7 m Central Africans were still in need of *aid* and 1.4 m. people were affected by food insecurity at the end of the year. Shortly before year's end, the UN OCHA humanitarian response plan had received $ 319.9 m, representing only 52% of total funding requirements (with the USA and the EU being the major donors). Humanitarian organisations complained of frequent targeting by armed groups.

Central African Republic in 2016

The transition phase after the overthrow of President François Bozizé in 2013 ended with presidential and legislative elections, but the new institutions barely had an influence on (in)security, and close to none in the eastern half of the country. Large parts of the territory were under the control of rebel movements, though infighting along ethnic (and no longer religious) lines clearly increased. UN peacekeepers were only partially successful in keeping the various armed groups at bay and became increasingly unpopular. The upsurge in violence clearly impinged on economic recovery.

Domestic Politics

A majority of both citizens and international partners were impatiently awaiting the end of the transitional period as the *transitional bodies*, including interim President Catherine Samba-Panza and her government, had lost most of their legitimacy over the preceding years. However, the first round of legislative elections on 30 January – held in parallel to the first round of the presidential elections – was marred by imperfections, mostly on the level of electoral administration, and had to be annulled early in the year. The results of the *presidential competition* were surprising to many observers. Neither the sons of former heads of states (Désiré Kolingba 12.0%, Jean-Serge Bokassa 6.1%, Sylvain Patassé-Ngakoutou 2.8%) nor the candidate of the oldest political party 'Mouvement pour la Libération du Peuple Centrafricain' (MLPC), Martin Ziguélé (11.4%), achieved the support they had hoped for, but two former prime ministers, Anicet-Georges Dologuélé and Archange-Faustin Touadéra, came top of the list with 23.7% and 19.1% of the votes respectively. Two other candidates (out of 30) had respectable results: the independent Charles-Armel Doubane (3.6%) and Jean-Michel Mandaba of

© KONINKLIJKE BRILL NV, LEIDEN, 2020 | DOI:10.1163/9789004436008_009

the 'Parti pour la Gouvernance Démocratique' (PGD; 3.1%). Past experience of high governmental responsibility was the only common factor shared by both the candidates who proceeded to the second round. Dologuélé had formed a party in 2013, the 'Union pour le Renouveau Centrafricain' (URCA), while Touadéra presented himself as an independent. When positioning themselves for the second round, to take place on 14 February, Touadéra played on his image as a modest technocrat, while poster images of Dologuélé bursting with self-confidence were omnipresent in the capital, Bangui. Dologuélé clearly had the support of many businessmen, as well as the official endorsement of former president Bozizé, and he also secured the backing of Kolingba, while Touadéra, most significantly, was able to enlist the support of the MLPC. In the end, Touadéra won the second round with a wide margin of 67.3% to 32.7%, according to provisional results announced on 20 February. Dologuélé at first tried to list irregularities in order to contest this outcome, but the gap between the votes was such that he accepted the result "for the sake of peace" and the Constitutional Court quickly endorsed the official result as given by the Electoral Commission on 1 March. Turnout fell only slightly from 62.5% in round 1 to 59.0% in round 2. Touadéra's inauguration on 30 March preceded the official end of the transition period by one day.

The re-run of the first round of *legislative elections* in parallel to the second round of the presidential elections produced clear victories in only 46 out of the 140 single-member constituencies. This meant that the contours of the post-transitional setup became clear only with the holding of the further postponed second round on 31 March, with results announced on 9 April. Touadéra's direct support in the National Assembly appeared limited in a highly fragmented parliament: his opponent Dologuélé could at least draw on his 13 URCA followers, while the 'Union Nationale pour la Démocratie et le Progrès', another new party, won the same number of seats. The parties that were arguably the best established fared moderately well, but experienced a geographically-based shrinking of their support: Kolingba's 'Rassemblement Démocratique Centrafricain' (RDC) was able to win ten seats (four of them in Basse Kotto prefecture), followed by Ziguélé's MLPC with nine seats (five of them in Ouham-Pendé). Bozizé's loosely organised 'Kwa na Kwa' party scored well, with seven seats. Twelve more parties received between one and four seats, while 56 independent candidates were elected, among them Anti-balaka leader Alfred Yekatom, who was under UN sanctions. Results in nine more constituencies were invalidated and partial re-elections had to be organised there. Only 11 women were elected.

Touadéra appointed Simplice Sarandji, his campaign manager and a professor at the University of Bangui, as prime minister on 6 April and Sarandji formed a *government* of 23 ministers on 12 April. With Bokassa as minister of public security and territorial administration, Doubane at Foreign Affairs and Joseph Yakete at the Defence Ministry, three presidential candidates who had supported Touadéra in the second round received meaningful recognition. Two close allies of Touadéra, Félix Moloua and Charles Lemasset, received the Economy and Communications portfolios, respectively, and some further official allies were represented by less well-known individuals, but Dologuélé's URCA also entered government. In contrast to all transitional governments (2013–16), not a single representative of an armed group was included. While the limited size of the government was meant to be a clear sign of modesty, Touadéra extended the size of the president's immediate circle of collaborators, including with some political heavyweights. General Antoine Gambi, chief of staff under Patassé, implicated in the coup against him and later sacked by Bozizé, was made the personal chief of staff at the Presidency. Equally controversial was the nomination of the versatile former minister Fidèle Gouandjika as special adviser. On 6 May, members of parliament elected Karim Meckassoua as Speaker with a simple majority (with Dologuélé and Ziguélé coming second and third). This was interpreted as a sign of reconciliation with the Muslim minority, which had at least partly backed the Séléka rebellion (though not Meckassoua, who had held several ministerial positions in the past).

With the main political institutions in place, Touadéra initiated a first round of consultations with representatives of armed movements on the *demobilisation, disarmament and reintegration* (DDR) process. All the major ex-Séléka factions – 'Front Populaire pour la Renaissance de la Centrafrique' (FPRC), 'Mouvement Patriotique pour la Centrafrique' (MPC) and 'Union pour la Paix en Centrafrique' (UPC) – resented their exclusion from government. They had demanded ministerial positions as a condition for their disarmament and now felt marginalised, while Touadéra stressed that DDR should come first. Presidential advisor Jean Willybiro-Sako was made a special coordinator for this dossier. On 24 August, Touadéra appointed members to an advisory and monitoring committee for the national DDR programme, including two members from the executive branch, one from the National Assembly, one from civil society, three from religious platforms, 28 from political-military groups, and five representatives of the international community. The president himself met with armed groups during visits to Bouar, Kaga-Bandoro and Bria; in addition, Willybiro-Sako met with 'Rassemblement Patriotique pour le Renouveau de la Centrafrique' (RPRC) and Anti-balaka representatives in Bambari. Most interlocutors expressed their interest in DDR, though expectations varied and were partly unrealistic. Nevertheless, on 3 November, the aforementioned committee unanimously adopted the national strategy on the matter in advance of the 17 November Brussels Donors Conference, at which resources in support of the plan were to be mobilised. Without transparency on budget allocations and entitlements in a full DDR programme, the UN Multidimensional Integrated Stabilization Mission in the CAR (MINUSCA) conducted so-called pre-DDR operations (in Bambari, Bangui, Birao, Bossangoa, Bouar, Bria, Kaga-Bandoro and Ndélé), reaching around 4,000 beneficiaries, who received food assistance and had to participate in short-term labour-intensive activities. Related to the slow process of DDR was the belated start of *security sector reform.* The Ministry of Defence had registered 7,478 members of the CAR armed forces, of whom 3,533 had been verified by MINUSCA as of mid-September. A joint task force of UNDP, MINUSCA, national police and gendarmerie undertook an identification exercise among the internal security forces, which resulted in the registration of 1,874 gendarmes and 1,154 police. In the same period, Touadéra created a presidential security unit, composed of some 175 personnel from the armed forces, police and gendarmerie. Their mission was the protection of residences of high-level government officials in Bangui.

After many postponements, a *reunification meeting of ex-Séléka factions* was held on 18–19 October in Bria, initiated by Nourredine Adam (FPRC). MINUSCA was overburdened with the arrival of between 1,000 and 1,500 armed men and was unable to maintain the status of Bria as a weapons-free zone, but no major incidents were reported. Neither the MPC leadership under Mahamat Al Khatim nor the UPC faction under Ali Darassa arrived for the meeting (according to them because Adam was on the UN sanctions list) and only the FPRC and RPRC signed a joint declaration. Even between those two factions, divisions remained quite obvious, the former being dominated by Runga, the latter by Goula, at loggerheads over the control of the sparsely populated north-east. However, the Bria declaration contained some significant formulations by condemning the continued persecution of minorities by Anti-balaka, allegedly armed by the government, and by calling for a partition of the country, with the north-east under rebel control. The meeting established a so-called High Supreme Council, with Nourredine Adam as president and Zacharia Damane as vice-president, and a National Council on Defence and Security with Abdoulaye Hissène as president. Significantly, the former leader and president of the FPRC, Michel Djotodia, did not take part and was not assigned any role. Observers had doubts as to whether Séléka could be reunified and regain the full strength it had in 2013.

Without tangible progress in DDR, the *security situation* remained volatile and worsened dramatically in the second half of the year. Conflict and security constellations varied from one region to the next, but few areas were constantly at full peace (arguably only the south-west). One hotspot was the capital, where the killing of a Muslim youth by a Christian youth led to inter-communal violence. When security forces detained 26 Muslim traders for days (18–24 June), it led to retaliatory action by the FPRC, who detained six police officers in the PK-5 neighbourhood of Bangui. MINUSCA peacekeepers tried in vain to free them by force on 20 June, killing at least six people. They were released only on 24 June – the same day a non-uniformed MINUSCA peacekeeper was killed. In a reconciliatory move, Touadéra hosted a Ramadan-related dinner on 27 June; he also attended the celebration of the Eid al-Adha holiday in PK-5. But symbolic behaviour was obviously of only limited use. On 12 August, most of the men of an FPRC contingent stationed in PK-5, including Abdoulaye Hissène and Haroun Gaye (the latter under UN sanctions), tried to flee Bangui and were immediately tracked by Anti-balaka, reportedly with the tacit support of civilian politicians. In PK-12, Sibut and Kemio, still close to the capital, clashes occurred. While national security forces had to withdraw due to a shortage of ammunition, MINUSCA's (late) intervention turned into a dramatic show-down with 11 FPRC members it had captured, some severely wounded, while others hiding in the bush later became victims of a man-hunt by Anti-balaka elements; still others were able to reach Séléka-controlled areas. This event not only affected MINUSCA's reputation but also impacted on the balance of power in the PK-5 area in Bangui, where infighting between Muslim self-help groups resulted in the death of two of their leaders. In October, the assassination of a high-ranking army officer and former guard of interim president Samba-Panza triggered a new round of inter-communal violence. The Anti-balaka movement was partly invigorated by the return on 3 August of Jean-Francis Bozizé, son of the former president and former defence minister, despite being wanted on an international arrest warrant for, inter alia, torture and embezzlement. Arrested by MINUSCA and handed over to the government, he was quickly set free again under hypothetical judicial surveillance. Bozizé Jr was clearly trying to reorganise the militant support base of the Bozizé family, potentially preparing for his father's return. While Bozizé Sr had openly supported Dologuélé, it was obvious that Touadéra had been more popular in this camp and this latent sympathy also made some government members quite relaxed about pursuing wanted Anti-balaka leaders, helping to freeze their assets and condemning their violent actions. In the same vein, calls for an end to the weapons embargo so that national security forces could be equipped became increasingly popular, and were supported, for example, by Defence Minister Bokassa. A former member of the Transitional National Council, Gervais Lakosso, organised protest actions against MINUSCA for their alleged passivity in the face of continued violence. On 24 October, a MINUSCA intervention against protesters resulted in four dead and 13 injured, including five peacekeepers.

The *north-west* was definitely not under government control. As a new factor, the MPC moved to the Paoua area in Ouham-Pendé prefecture and formed an alliance with former enemies of the 'Révolution et Justice' militia, which resulted from late January onwards in the occupation or burning of villages close by. An attack attributed to 'ex-Séléka' created panic in Ngaoundaye on 16 June. Further sporadic clashes occurred between, on the one hand, Anti-balaka and the 'Front Démocratique pour le Peuple Centrafricain' (FDPC) and, on the other, Fulani pastoralists and those movements claiming to protect them, such as the 2015-founded 'Retour, Réclamation et Réhabilitation' (3R), the FPRC and the MPC. A rare positive development came in July, when the FDPC released two different groups of hostages and expressed readiness to be disarmed. From April onwards, confrontations between Anti-balaka and Fulani and between 3R and non-Fulani civilians around Bocaranga and Koui increased, with casualties rising, and HRW documented the killing of at least 50 civilians at the end of November. HRW held 3R under 'general' Sidiki Abbas responsible for the displacement of at least 17,000 people (14,000 around Bocaranga, 3,000 on the border with Cameroon).

The *centre* of the country (Ouaka and Nana-Grébizi préfectures) looked even more tense, and in particular Bambari, where a dissident Arab faction of the UPC under Abdoulaye Faya clashed with those loyal to UPC leader Ali Darassa, who repeatedly stated that his mission was to defend Fulani interests. In clashes on 4 July, at least 14 UPC combatants were killed. Thirty-seven dissidents sought shelter in the MINUSCA camp for seven weeks. A first convoy evacuating them to Kaga-Bandoro was stopped in Grimari by Anti-balaka fighters, potentially manipulated by the local district officer (sous-préfet), and had to return to Bambari. Eventually, most UPC defectors were transferred by aircraft to Kaga-Bandoro on 2 September with a view to their early demobilisation. Darassa now consolidated his control over the area, and also over the diamond mining site of Nzako further east in Mbomou prefecture. The UPC was responsible for a number of escalations in October, including the killing of two village chiefs. Shortly afterwards, on 27 October, UPC combatants killed 11 people in the village of Berima and then, on 29 October, six gendarmes sent to investigate the crime. In response, Anti-balaka groups erected road-blocks in a Bambari neighbourhood under their control. However, the Anti-balaka movement was split on the national level between a faction under a degree of control by Maxime Mokom and a faction claiming to be loyal to Edouard Ngaïssona, with the latter faction dominant in Ouaka prefecture. Rather surprisingly, the FPRC and Anti-balaka formed an alliance against the UPC. The UPC ran illegal detention centres and exercised other state-like functions in Ouaka; it also organised forced marriages and used child-soldiers. By the end of the year, new atrocities had been attributed to the UPC, including the execution of over 60 civilians and captured fighters in November and December in or close to Bakala, which also led to new internal displacement. As if this were not enough, a new militia formed on 4 August. The 'Mouvement de Résistance pour la Défense de la Patrie' had some overlaps with the Anti-balaka and issued an ultimatum to MINUSCA to arrest Darassa by 4 October. After that date, the MRDP claimed the shooting at a MINUSCA convoy on 12 October, injuring five peacekeepers (two assailants and one civilian were killed), and it threatened more action, particularly to bring about the departure of the Mauritanian contingent of MINUSCA from Bambari. Kaga-Bandoro was also the scene of serious fighting and looting, in one instance leaving at least 37 civilians and 12 ex-Séléka fighters dead and more than 50 people injured in an attack on an IDP centre. Approximately 6,500 IDPs sought refuge around MINUSCA facilities; both the MPC and the FRSP denied involvement, though fighters were identified as 'ex-Séléka'.

In the *east*, Bria became a further hot spot by the end of November, when about 85 civilians were killed, 76 wounded and nearly 11,000 displaced due to a confrontation between the FPRC and the UPC. Finally, the *south-east* saw an extension of Lord's Resistance Army (LRA) activities. According to the LRA Crisis Tracker, over the year 750 civilians were abducted (and 18 killed) in 106 incidents in the CAR, a steep rise compared with 2015. It was mostly towns in Mboumou, Haut-Mboumou and Haute-Kotto prefectures that experienced LRA attacks.

In light of an obviously weak government and the impression of on-going impunity, it seemed essential that the law to establish a Special Criminal Court signed in 2015 should be implemented. Human rights NGOs estimated that such a Special Court would cost $ 40 m for the first five years. Of that amount, only $ 5 m were raised. Earlier, an initial budget of $ 7 m for starting the Court's operations was drawn up. MINUSCA began to develop a list of persons suspected of serious crimes.

Foreign Affairs

The CAR remained a constant item on the UNSC agenda. On 27 January, by resolution 2262, the UNSC prolonged the comprehensive sanctions regime, including a full arms embargo and targeted sanctions including travel bans and asset freezing, plus an extension of the mandate of the panel of experts, all until the end of January 2017. Furthermore, by resolution 2331, the UNSC decided on 26 July to extend the mandate of *MINUSCA* until 15 November 2017. MINUSCA operated close to the mandated limit of 10,750 military personnel, including 480 military observers and staff officers and 2,080 police personnel. However, the mission faced several critical situations in which it had to deploy force, and faced harsh criticism from various political actors for either not being impartial or being inactive. Past allegations of sexual harassment also kept peacekeepers on the radar of human rights organisations. Responding to reports of atrocities carried out in the country of origin, UN headquarters announced that Burundi's police units (280) within MINUSCA would not be replaced at the end of their assignment in September.

Other external actors faced similar problems. On 7 June, *Uganda People's Defence Force* (UPDF) troops serving under the AU-mandated Regional Task Force (RTF) met violent demonstrators in Zémio after the controversial arrest of a civilian over a stolen UPDF weapon. One Ugandan soldier was reportedly stabbed in the event; in retaliation a civilian was killed by a UPDF soldier. On 25 August, an LRA commando killed a UPDF soldier and wounded two in an attack 60 km north-east of Zémio. On 20 May, the government of Uganda announced that it would withdraw from the RTF mission by the end of the year; but it did not do so.

Touadéra's inauguration ceremony on 30 March was attended by just two heads of state, Denis Sassou Nguesso (Congo) in his capacity as international mediator in the CAR crisis and Equatorial Guinea's Obiang Nguema, but also by two French ministers, Foreign Minister Jean-Marc Ayrault and Defence Minister Jean-Yves le Drian. The official *end of the transition period* had several consequences. With the restoration of a constitutional order, the CAR was readmitted as a full member of the AU on 7 April (after having been suspended in March 2013). It also meant that the mediation role of CEEAC (and Sassou Nguesso) was terminated. Le Drian announced the *termination of the French Sangaris mission*, arguably the most effective unit among all international peacekeepers. Touadéra met French President François Hollande in Paris before and after his inauguration, on 20 March and 20 April, and in Bangui on 13 May, and tried in vain to get guarantees for an extension. Visiting Bangui again on 31 October, le Drian declared the end of the Sangaris mission with its now 900 soldiers, but promised that France would stay engaged via contributions to MINUSCA and the EU Military Training Mission in the CAR (EUTM RCA), with about 350 soldiers. The EUTM RCA, with a nominal strength of 170 personnel and a budget of € 12.4 m in the current year, had a mandate to support the armed forces with strategic advice, education for officers and non-commissioned officers, and operational training. The EU Council adopted the programme on 16 July, with its first mandate expiring in September 2018. Touadéra had a busy schedule with overseas trips, including to Rome on 18 April (visiting FAO headquarters, the Pope, and Italy's President Sergio Matarella), and New York on 8–10 June to attend the UNSC and meet with Ban Ki-moon.

In terms of *relations in Africa*, Toudéra clearly privileged neighbouring countries. Starting with short-term trips immediately after his election, Touadéra visited Chad, Cameroon and the Sudan at least twice, and also Congo, the DRC and Equatorial Guinea. Foreign fighters in various rebel groups originated mostly from *Chad* and *Sudan*, but both governments looked ready to cooperate with the new CAR government. Chadian authorities complained about incursions by armed groups from the CAR. Quite obviously, however, rebel leader Nourredine Adam was able to travel freely to southern Chad, despite a UN travel ban. New concerns that remnants of the 'Mouvement pour la Libération du Congo' (MLC) were again able to operate from Bangui were voiced after a former commander, Freddy Libeba Baongoli, was seen in the capital and later vowed in a video message to oust Kabila by force. In the ICC case against MLC leader Jean-Pierre Bemba, the verdict was finally declared on 21 March. He was found guilty of crimes against humanity, confirming that he had had effective authority and control over the forces that committed such crimes in Bangui in 2002. On 21 June, Bemba was sentenced to 18 years' imprisonment; he appealed against this verdict.

At the end of the year, *Cameroon* was hosting most of the CAR's refugees (around 260,000), around 7,000 of whom had arrived during the year. Most were concentrated in the sparsely populated eastern region, where refugees from the CAR now represented around one-fifth of the overall population. Illegal smuggling activities – diamonds for weapons – threatened to destabilise the area, with Cameroonian officials probably involved in illegal activities. FDPC rebels operated on both sides of the border. The two other main nations hosting refugees from the CAR were the DRC (103,000) and Chad (71,000). A return intentions survey carried out in December on behalf of UNHCR revealed that 73% of CAR refugees did not intend to go home, citing security concerns.

On 5 December, the *UN Panel of Experts* issued its final report, with many details on the continuation of the war economy. The experts also analysed the growing unpopularity of MINUSCA not only among the population, but also in government circles. Infractions of the sanctions regime were frequent, by both individuals and national authorities, and also by African governments (particularly South Africa, Kenya and Chad) inviting or allowing individuals under sanctions to enter their territory. During the year, Joseph Kony (LRA), believed to be on CAR territory, and his two sons Ali and Salim were put on the UN sanctions list.

Socioeconomic Development

On 20 July, the IMF's Executive Board approved a three-year SDR 83.6 m (about $115.8 m) arrangement under the *ECF*. $ 17.4 m of this was earmarked for immediate disbursement to restore macroeconomic stability. This decision was based on the recently concluded Article IV consultations. In the final report, IMF staff presented details of a still sombre picture. This included public debt, which had increased markedly from 23.5% of GDP (2012) to 48.5% (2015), as a result of both the significant fall in GDP and a rise in domestic payment arrears. *Payment arrears* were also accumulated towards a number of bilateral creditors (including recently China, India and the Saudi Development Fund). Capacities to address manifest management problems were critically low. The most relevant ministries (Finance and Budget, Planning, and International Cooperation) and the Institute of Statistics and Prices were understaffed, poorly equipped and working under difficult conditions, '"including a lack of sufficient energy to power computers and office equipment". IMF staff identified three risks to its joint programme with the authorities: absence of political agreement with armed groups, limited experience of the new government, and delayed provision of financial assistance from the international community. The last, according to the IMF, would jeopardise critical reforms, including in the security sector. In fact, the deteriorating security situation was given as major explanation for the revision towards the end of the year of initially optimistic projections. *GDP growth*, initially projected at 5.2%, was estimated at 4.5% in December, while inflation went up from 4.0%to 5.1% – lower than the African average, but also significantly higher than the convergence rate of 3% set by CEMAC.

The weakness of private operators was equally evident, particularly the *financial sector*, the smallest in CEMAC. The IMF termed it "largely underdeveloped" and saw it playing a limited role in supporting the economy. Only about 1% of the population held a bank account and 0.5% had access to credit.

The National Assembly passed a *revised budget* (of CFAfr 259.2 bn in expenses with a CFA 49.2 bn deficit) on 2 October to account for increased spending. According to the new budget, domestic revenue should be kept at 8% of GDP (estimated at $ 1.7 bn), while primary spending would be slightly reduced to 11.3% of GDP. Despite critical discussions, the law was passed by a large majority.

The critical *donor meeting* on 17 November in Brussels came at a moment of waning confidence in the new authorities. However, donor commitments reached a total of € 2.1 bn, about one quarter more than the government had expected. The European Commission pledged € 409 m, while EU member states made additional pledges amounting to € 298 m (for 2017–21). Touadéra admitted having noted some reservations about the government's ability to implement the recovery plan, but committed himself to ensuring that all funds were properly accounted for.

The partial lifting of a *diamond sales embargo* within the Kimberley Process, allowing the export of diamonds produced in the western part of the country, originally only from Berberati, was extended in September to include Boda, Carnot and Nola as 'compliant zones'. The export of rough diamonds from those areas resumed, while export from the eastern production zones (under rebel control) remained banned. However, it was obvious that a major part of the diamonds produced was smuggled out of the country. One indication was that a suspiciously strong and growing number of probably fake Kimberley Process certificates from Cameroon had been issued in previous years, exceeding the total official annual production of Cameroon and most probably stemming from the CAR.

The *humanitarian situation* remained problematic. In a press release on 28 November, the UN Office for the Coordination of Humanitarian Affairs (OCHA) stated that nearly half of the population were still in need of humanitarian assistance. A cholera outbreak in central CAR in summer killed at least 16 people (66 cases were confirmed). By 31 December, only slightly fewer than in 2015, some 460,000 refugees, plus 410,000 IDPs were waiting for improved conditions to return to their home regions.

Central African Republic in 2017

The population faced another disastrous year with the number of IDPs and refugees continuing to increase as a result of renewed fighting in various parts of the country; food insecurity hit nearly half of the population. The elected government in conjunction with international actors managed to secure the vital Bangui-Douala corridor, but fully controlled only the south-west. In the centre, the south-east and the north-west, new deadly confrontations, often involving unexpected coalitions of armed movements, could not be prevented, even by international peacekeepers who sometimes faced outright popular hostility. Efforts to prepare the justice system to deal with past crimes against humanity were taken, but did not yet yield results.

Domestic Politics

President Archange-Faustin Touadéra met with criticism from many quarters when he had little to show in terms of economic progress and security after one year in office. Faced with half a dozen policy guidelines, some observers wondered what the government's vision for restoring stability was and raised doubts as to whether there even was one. A core issue was the official attitude towards the numerous armed movements that continued to threaten peace and rarely behaved responsibly. Touadéra clearly favoured an inclusive approach, potentially because he did not have the means to confront rebel groups effectively. On 12 September, he carried out a *major reshuffle* of his government, appointing 16 new ministers and raising the number of portfolios within the cabinet from 23 to 34. The return of Marie-Noëlle Koyara, who had been the first female minister of defence during the transition period, to that same post was potentially a positive surprise. More significant, however, was

© KONINKLIJKE BRILL NV, LEIDEN, 2020 | DOI:10.1163/9789004436008_010

the fact that some new ministers were linked to armed movements: Energy Minister Gontran Djono Ahaba, the nephew of former warlord president Michel Djotodia, and Water and Forestry Minister Lambert Mokove Lissane were clearly seen as representatives of the Ex-Séléka movement within government. Equally represented was now the opposing anti-Balaka movement with Government Secretary Jean-Alexandre Dedet and Culture and Tourism Minister Jacob Mokpem Bionli. Retaining his position, Prime Minister Simplice Sarandji was quoted as saying, "For me they are all Central Africans", to justify the inclusion of rebels in the government. As a side-effect of this move, government expenditure was clearly set to rise.

In fact, both government and UN peacekeepers were unable to prevent or stop *on-going armed conflicts*, at first in the centre of the country. Since November 2016, two former components of the Séléka alliance, the 'Front Populaire pour la Renaissance de la Centrafrique' (FRPC) and the 'Union pour la Paix en Centrafrique' (UPC), had repeatedly clashed in or around Bambari. The FPRC was seen as completely opportunistic in its choices of partners, who included its former opponents, the Anti-Balaka movements, while the UPC was clearly linking up with sometimes very vulnerable, and sometimes violent and armed Fulani groups. On 12 February, the UN Multidimensional Integrated Stabilization Mission in the CAR (MINUSCA) intervened to halt the advance of the FPRC coalition, killing the FPRC chief of staff, Joseph Zoundéko. MINUSCA obtained the withdrawal of militia structures from the city, including the UPC headquarters under Ali Darassa, and the local anti-Balaka chief, Gaétan Boadé, also left Bambari. MINUSCA then declared Bambari a "city free from armed groups". Violence declined in this key city, but the moves resulted in a *transfer of conflict further east*, with several attacks recorded on Bakouma, Nzako and Zémio. An upsurge in violence was recorded in May, hitting mostly the provincial capitals of Bangassou (with more than 100 killed) and Bria, but also Alindao (188 died here alone according to HRW, which also documented 25 cases of rape), Mobaye and later again Zémio, often against armed

Fulani cattle herders and Anti-Balaka groups loosely allied to the FRPC. In Bria, in-fighting between the factions of this alliance resulted in an upsurge of 73,000 IDPs in May and June. Between 20 and 23 June, over 80 civilians died in these battles. In a particularly bloody confrontation in the town of Gambo in early August, Anti-Balaka elements attacked UPC and armed Fulani individuals, who retaliated by targeting a local health centre; more than 100 civilians were killed, including International Committee of the Red Cross volunteers. On 18 October, Anti-Balaka militia attacked the Fulani village of Pombolo, killing at least 26 civilians; this was preceded by an attack on Kembe eight days earlier resulting in a similar death toll.

The second most dangerous zone was the area between Batangafo and Kaga Bandoro (in the north). Here the 'Mouvement Patriotique pour la Centrafrique' (MPC) and Anti-Balaka groups fought for control of Batangafo. In December, two villages in the vicinity were largely destroyed by MPC troops, leading to the displacement of some 24,000 civilians. Further to the west, at the end of the year the newly established 'Mouvement National pour la Libération de la Centrafrique' (MNLC; a recent MPC splinter group) clashed with the locally strong 'Révolution et Justice' (RJ) movement in and around Paoua. RJ and the hitherto rival Anti-Balaka fighters joined forces to counter the MNLC, but also targeted civilian Muslim communities, killing four civilians; the MNLC burned down entire villages in retaliation. Tens of thousands of people were internally displaced and up to 500 people were killed.

But tensions were also high in many other places. While autochthony discourses and interreligious animosity played some role in individual outbursts of violence, it was rather the *competition for access to valuable natural resources or trade routes* that remained the key driver of violence among the armed groups. Even within the armed movements, significant violence was used to settle scores between local commanders, On 7–8 December, rival factions of the FPRC clashed in Ippy (in the centre of the country), resulting in an undetermined number of casualties and the displacement of over 15,000 civilians. This terminated a phase of relative peace that had prevailed after the 'Rassemblement des Républicains' (RDR), an Anti-Balaka faction, had signed an agreement with the FPRC, MPC and UPC in October. In mid-December, UPC elements reportedly killed Gaétan Bouadé, the RDR leader.

In contrast, the security situation in the capital *Bangui* improved somewhat after the last escalation in February, when a local militia leader was killed, leading to further killings in retaliation. It was mostly in the third arrondissement of Bangui that militia members clashed in internal power struggles and competition over illegally imposed taxes; in one obscure event a grenade exploded on 11 November, killing four people.

Although pilot projects were started, the *implementation of DDR* made little progress – to no one's surprise in the circumstances. The FPRC, one of the most important movements, even suspended its participation. The government and the donor community, with MINUSCA as the main implementer, engaged in all sorts of DDR, while in parallel working to build up new and reliable national security forces. In November, MINUSCA removed the mostly Fulani 3R ('Retour, Reclamation, Rehabilitation') forces under the command of General Sidiki Abass from Bocaranga and the MPC from nearby Bang. On 30 October, Defence Minister Koyara issued a concept paper for the training of the national armed forces by the EU Military Training Mission (EUTM-RCA) and, on 18 November, President Touadéra signed two decrees on the organisation of the 'Forces Armées Centrafricaines' (FACA) and the general staff. Seventy FACA soldiers trained by the EUTM-RCA were deployed to Obo in November as a first detachment, and 72 further FACA soldiers were sent to Paoua to work alongside MINUSCA.

Considerable efforts were deployed to reach an inclusive *peace agreement*. The Catholic Sant'Egidio community organised intensive talks in Rome and Foreign Affairs Minister Charles Armel Doubane and President Touadéra's political advisor, Georges-Isidore-Alphose Dibert, eventually signed a so-called 'Entente de

Sant'Egidio' on behalf of the government, as did representatives of 13 armed movements. Of the important players, only the 3R movement was not present. It is worth noting that four of the major civilian political parties co-signed the document along with the vice president of the National Assembly. The document called, inter alia, for an immediate ceasefire, respect for the elected authorities and the acceptance of the political-military groups as part of security sector reform and the reconstruction process. The possibility of an amnesty was alluded to, in stark contrast to the peace roadmap presented by the National Assembly to the government in May, which had excluded amnesties for war crimes. The document was clearly not worth the paper it was written on: only a day after the signing of the agreement, nearly 100 people were killed in Bria in clashes between the FPRC and Anti-Balaka fighters. Taking the fragmentation of groups into account, it was much more realistic to engage in local peace agreements as those signing a paper would then also commit to their words. An agreement between the 3R and local Anti-Balaka groups was signed in Bouar on 15 December, and local authorities in Bria, supported by MINUSCA, launched a road map for peace in Haute-Kotto on 19 December.

The (re-)establishment of *state authority* was one of the main goals of both the government and MINUSCA. The progressive deployment of trained FACA battalions was only one element of this strategy. On 8 September, a concept note was published and four days later Touadéra appointed new prefects to all 16 prefectures, nine of them with a military background (and none of them Muslim). In October, he corrected that balance somewhat: among the 71 sub-prefects (i.e. district officers), various rebel movements and the Muslim community were represented. At year's end, 14 of the 16 prefects and 63 of the 71 sub-prefects were installed. The FPRC and MPC were initially opposed to the redeployment of state authorities in Bamingui-Bangoran, Vakaga and Nana-Grebizi prefectures. In some cases, extensive consultation with armed groups preceded the deployment, showing the nature of the local balance of power.

Fighting impunity was another important challenge; both a restoration of the formal *justice system* and establishing internationally sponsored transitional justice organs were on the agenda. On 23 February, President Touadéra signed a decree naming a military judge from the neighbouring DRC, Colonel Toussaint Muntazini Mukimapa, as the prosecutor of the Special Criminal Court (SCC). In May, two female international investigating judges were appointed, as were five national judges, but the SCC was still not operational by year's end. In parallel, 19 of the 24 first instance and appellate courts started to function, though with reduced capacity. In the last two months of the year, eight Anti-Balaka members were sentenced by a court in Bouar (in the west) to up to 20 years' imprisonment for criminal association, unlawful possession of homemade arms, murder and theft. On 11 September, President Touadéra created a preparatory committee for a truth, justice, reparations and reconciliation commission, which had been asked for in the aforementioned Sant'Egidio declaration. On the other hand, the government did little to implement an asset freeze for a number of individuals, who were still able to receive their state salaries despite being under international sanctions.

The *Lord's Resistance Army* (LRA) continued to pose a threat in the south-east. In late October, the group stepped up its attacks on villages. AI, referring to other NGOs, calculated that there were 113 attacks, 12 civilian casualties and 362 kidnappings over the year. The withdrawal of Ugandan forces (which had officially fought the LRA) ended in August, and this also enabled various Ex-Séléka factions to gain ground in the south-east.

Foreign Affairs

In the competition for international public attention, the CAR again fell into the background compared to other crisis areas including Syria and Mali, but arguably also Yemen and Myanmar (with the

Rohingya crisis), which had consequences for levels of assistance. Potentially, it was in this context that UN Under-Secretary-General for Humanitarian Affairs Stephen O'Brien repeated the warning of precursors to *genocide*, although no criteria for genocide were given, and neither was this a mainly interreligious conflict. It was true that in individual cases mosques and Muslim traders were targeted by some armed groups: in one instance, Anti-Balaka attacked a mosque in Bangassou on 13 May, killing the town's imam, amongst others. The Catholic Church in the town subsequently hosted 1,500 Muslim civilians in their premises. But there was certainly not any systematic move to kill entire religious or ethnic groups on a national scale.

At the margins of the UN General Assembly session, UN Secretary General António Guterres co-presided with President Touadéra and the chairperson of the AU at a high-level meeting on 19 September on the political, security and humanitarian situation in the CAR. At a press conference, Touadéra deplored the departure of France's Operation Sangaris in 2016, and also the withdrawal starting in April–May of about 2,000 US and Ugandan forces that formed part of the AU-led Regional Task Force that was fighting the LRA. Guterres also visited the CAR on 24–27 October as the first country in a series of further visits to peacekeeping operations worldwide.

MINUSCA peacekeepers continued to be met with hostility and were not unopposed even within government. The local population in Bangui repeatedly attacked staff and property. On 10 May, Anti-Balaka allegedly kidnapped and killed peacekeepers in the deadliest attack on a MINUSCA convoy since the establishment of the mission. Five peacekeepers were killed and ten were injured on the road between Bangassou and Rafai. On 24 November, a crowd threw stones at UN vehicles after a fatal road accident attributed to MINUSCA: three peacekeepers were injured and three MINUSCA vehicles destroyed in the event. On 9 December, a rocket was launched into the MINUSCA camp in Kaga Bandoro, probably as part of the protest against the arrival of the new prefect; nobody was killed or injured. Facing the upsurge of violence, the UNSC renewed the

MINUSCA mandate on 15 November for another year and authorised an increase of the troop ceiling by 900 to a maximum of 11,650 military personnel in order to bolster one core task in particular – the protection of civilians. Accusations of misconduct remained common. Most significant was that, in June, Congo was pushed to withdraw its 629 troops in response to sexual abuse allegations. A leaked memo stated that six accusatory letters had been sent to the battalion commander regarding not only alleged sexual abuse, but also fuel trafficking and lack of discipline. Several allegations of sexual abuse dating back a number of years involving French forces deployed under Operation Sangaris were dismissed by French judicial authorities.

In search of international support, Touadéra did not limit himself to the CAR's traditional partners. A state visit to *France* on 25 September did not bring about new prospects of military cooperation. He also met with *EU* High Representative Federica Mogherini and President of the European Parliament (EP) Antonio Tajani in Brussels on 22 November ahead of the EP conference 'Towards a renewed partnership with Africa', in which he also participated. At the margins of the event Touadéra called for material support for the SCC.

Less conventional was his meeting with Russian Foreign Minister Sergei Lavrov on 9 October in Sotchi (Russia). In November and December, *Russia* lobbied the UNSC to lift the arms embargo on the CAR in order to equip the FACA with small arms and light weapons. This had been a constant request from Bangui authorities during the transition period but it had not been favourably received by most international partners, who did not trust the FACA. This assessment clearly changed with the progressive training of new FACA personnel by the EUTM-RCA and an exemption to the arms embargo was granted after reinforced security on warehouses was promised. Russia began almost immediately with the first shipment of arms for 1,300 soldiers including, inter alia, 900 pistols, 5,200 assault-rifles, 840 Kalashnikovs and 270 missile-launchers, plus ammunition. Russia also signalled its readiness to train the FACA on these weapons.

Within Africa, Touadéra made notable visits to neighbouring countries that had at least tacitly supported some rebel movements in the past. Most prominent was a trip to *Chad* on 29 June, where he met also AU President Alpha Condé of Guinea and the chairperson of the AU Commission Moussa Faki Mahamat (from Chad) alongside Chad's President Déby. There was press speculation that Touadéra was put under pressure on this occasion to issue amnesties to rebel leaders. A new *African Initiative for Peace and Reconciliation* in the CAR, established at the AU summit on 30–31 January, led to the adoption of a new 'roadmap to peace' by a ministerial conference held in Libreville (Gabon) on 17 July. The document was signed by representatives of the CAR government (Foreign Minister Doubane), the AU, CEEAC, ICGLR, Angola, Chad, Congo and Gabon. The roadmap was quite vague and did not provide for clear milestones. It claimed to include the contents of the previous (failed) attempt to establish a peace accord by Sant'Egidio in Rome, but clearly was meant to put African actors in the driver's seat for future negotiations. Subsequently, France affirmed that the African Initiative and this roadmap would constitute the main framework for a political solution, while the UN stressed the need for coordination with MINUSCA. All those efforts looked sterile as long as all the armed movements remained internally fragmented – self-nominated leaders could often speak only for a battalion of fighters. Chad was a key player in this new turn of events. In November, a National Assembly delegation went to N'Djamena and signed a parliamentary cooperation agreement. Touadéra participated at the CEMAC summit in N'Djamena on 31 October and he also visited *Sudan* on 10–11 December. Together with the presidents of Niger and Djibouti, Touadéra was one of the few African heads of state to come to Kigali for Rwandan President Kagame's inauguration ceremony on 18 August. On his return trip, he was accompanied by 40 of the 200 FACA soldiers trained by the Rwandan army. Touadéra, accompanied

by Defence Minister Koyara and Chief of Staff General Luc Ngai-
fei visited *Equatorial Guinea* at the end of the training phase of 144
FACA soldiers on 28 October, mostly to witness a demonstration of
their newly acquired military skills in the presence of President Obiang Nguema Mbasogo.

Socioeconomic Developments

GDP *growth* was slower than expected at around 4% (IMF projec-
tion), so that the losses resulting from years of turmoil (2012/13)
were still not recovered. The on-going violence in parts of the country significantly hampered agricultural production. Insecurity and
repeated displacement led to a 58 % decline in crop production and
increased food prices. Roughly every second person was in a food-
insecure situation. The rare good news was that the economically
central Bangui-Douala (Cameroon) corridor remained open, en-
abling a projected growth in export volume of 17.7%. Timber, cotton
and official diamond exports saw significant increases. Nevertheless,
there was little reason for optimism.

The upsurge of violence, first in the south-east and towards the
end of the year in the north-west, led to an increase in the number of *IDPs*, bringing the total to 688,700 – a 60% increase compared with 2016. The number of *refugees* increased by 26% to over
545,000 hosted in neighbouring countries, although 45,000 refugees
from earlier episodes of war returned to their villages of origin. This
meant that, by year's end, the overall number of those forcibly displaced was higher than ever. Humanitarian assistance was stepped
up, but the official humanitarian response plan of the UN's Office
for the Coordination of Humanitarian Affairs was underfunded
(61.3 % of the needs were not covered). One particular problem was
the dangerous work environment for humanitarian assistance: during the year, 14 aid workers were killed and 297 humanitarian workers were temporarily relocated because of the lack of security.

On 15 December, the IMF's executive board completed the third review under the *ECF* arrangement. Most importantly, this exercise enabled the disbursement of SDR (special drawing right) 28.41 m (about $ 40.2 m). The difficulties of running a reform agenda in parallel with efforts to gradually restore security in additional urban centres – and not only Bangui – were acknowledged. Overall, the IMF expressed satisfaction with the authorities' efforts in many fields, which even led to the approval of an augmentation of the ECF by SDR 38.99 m (about $ 55.1 m). As important was the assessment of needs as part of the national strategy for recovery and peace, as well as for a more solid backing of economic growth.

One source of concern was the high risk of *debt distress*. An updated so-called debt sustainability analysis suggested that the government should rely on grant financing with strict limitations on highly concessional financing for critical projects only.

State *revenue growth* in 2016 and 2017 was lower than projected, close to the African average of 2.2% of GDP. The state was able to reduce some of its domestic debt arrears. However, it was clear that only a higher productivity and income from taxes and customs would help matters. On 22 June, Global Witness published a report ('A Game of Stones') that described the continued possibilities for smuggled *diamonds* to fund armed movements in the CAR. The government rejected the report only a few days later and stressed the importance of diamond exports for economic recovery. In fact, many sources in the report predated the newly established policies, but it was undisputed that a good part of the diamond production left the country illegally. The readmission of diamond exports produced in so-called green zones under government control also led to a slow upturn in legal diamond exports as part of the processes foreseen in the so-called Kimberley Process. The World Diamond Council, an important body of the worldwide diamond industry, officially reaffirmed its support for efforts to prevent the trade in conflict diamonds originating from the CAR. The Ministry of Mining and MINUSCA undertook a joint mission to Berberati, a green zone designated by the Kimberley Process, to explore possibilities for national oversight and taxation of income generated by the illicit exploitation of natural resources. On 20 July, the General Court of the EU upheld an asset freeze imposed on two Belgian-based diamond companies that had procured diamonds from the CAR. It was clear that the main stakeholders in the war economy could count on partners outside the country.

Central African Republic in 2018

Both the domestic and international support base of the government appeared volatile. President Faustin-Archange Touadéra tried to extend his power base by creating his own political party, thereby sidelining former allies. A visible extension of Russian influence met with distrust by more traditional external partners of the country. Violence and insecurity haunted not only the inhabitants of Bangui but also a majority of prefectures, particularly in the first half of the year and again towards the end. Some of the major armed groups managed to consolidate their power bases, including by fixing zones of influence. Taxing the cattle trade became a major source of income for armed groups, adding to the benefits of smuggling natural resources.

Domestic Politics

President Touadéra enacted minor but significant changes of *government*. On 13 April, Jean-Serge Bokassa, son of Jean-Bédel Bokassa (president and later self-appointed emperor, 1966–79) was sacked from his position as minister of territorial administration and decentralisation. Among the reasons cited were repeated absences (from office, cabinet meetings, and official ceremonies). But reports had it also that he was at loggerheads with the president over the decision to put at the disposal of Russian military advisors his late father's estate of Berengo, located some 80 km south-west of the capital, Bangui. Rumours had it that he had already resigned in protest prior to his dismissal. Bokassa was not replaced in his position. With the dismissal of Charles Armel Doubane from his position as foreign minister on 14 December, Touadéra sacked a further competitor of the 2015/16 presidential race who had allied with him before the second round. Bokassa had received 6.1% and Doubane 3.6% of

© KONINKLIJKE BRILL NV, LEIDEN, 2020 | DOI:10.1163/9789004436008_011

the votes in the first round. Doubane was replaced by a newcomer, Sylvie Baïpo Témon, raising the number of female ministers from four to five.

Touadéra made efforts to reorganise his power base by creating his own *party*, the 'Mouvement Coeurs Unis' (MCU, United Hearts Movement) at an official first congress in November, when prime minister Simplice Sarandji became national executive secretary. Consequently, the importance credited to the 'Mouvement pour la Libération du Peuple Centrafricain' (MLPC), the oldest established party and most prominent supporter of the president, became questionable. Third-placed candidate Martin Ziguélé had also supported Touadéra in the run-off in 2016. Former prime minister Jean Edouard Koyambounou (MLPC) therefore asked for a redefinition of the alliance that his party had agreed to back then (which terms were, however, never disclosed to the public). Evidently, Touadéra was trying to become independent of his former allies, but his own popularity was also limited, as could be witnessed on National Day (1 December), when large-scale public ceremonies were boycotted by several opposition parties and the Catholic Church in protest against the inadequate response to recent attacks by armed groups against IDPs.

Tensions between the executive and legislative branches of the government had started already in the preceding year. President Touadéra in fact distrusted the *National Assembly*'s speaker, Abdou Karim Meckassoua, a very experienced former minister and equally candidate in the last presidential race. In particular, Meckassoua was credited with having established good relations with Paris. But on 26 October, a two-thirds majority of members voted to remove Meckassoua, who stood accused of misconduct. He was the highest-ranking Muslim in an official position, and his removal from office triggered angry reactions in his constituency (in Bangui, including the Muslim PK5 neighbourhood), but also by some Séléka representatives, although he had never been their supporter. Meckassoua was replaced by another Muslim, Laurent Ngon-Baba. The National

Assembly was the scene of a spectacular arrest only three days later, when anti-Balaka leader and MP Alfred Yekatom (aka 'Rambo') twice discharged his firearm in parliament, creating panic. He was immediately arrested by a gendarmerie squad and surrendered to the ICC after it issued a warrant on 11 November. Yekatom's lawyer claimed that thereby "international justice has stabbed the Central African justice with the help of local authorities". A second MP, Thierry Georges Vackat, was arrested at the same time as Yekatom, and weapons were found in his vehicle.

Transferred to The Hague on 17 November, Yekatom appeared for the first time before Pre-Trial Chamber II on 23 November, accused of war crimes and crimes against humanity committed between December 2013 and August 2014. His long-time rival within the anti-Balaka movement, Patrice-Edouard Ngaïssona, was arrested on 12 December in Paris. One of the critical sectors of state weakness was in fact the *judiciary*. It was obvious that the government preferred that Yekatom, who would have been both an embarrassing and dangerous prison inmate, stand trial in The Hague rather than in Bangui. Notwithstanding, on 4 June, the National Assembly had ratified a law creating the long-prepared Special Criminal Court, which theoretically would deal with cases like the aforementioned in the future. The Special Criminal Court held its inaugural session on 22 October, but it only issued its prosecution strategy on 4 December. Some work had already been done. In January, a somewhat prominent anti-Balaka leader, Rodrigue Ngaibona (alias 'General Andjilo'), was sentenced to life imprisonment in the Bangui criminal court. In day-to-day practice, the judiciary managed to resume sessions in places like Bouar and Bossangoa, years after they had been suspended, but this was only a hopeful start, and much more was needed to inspire confidence in state-sponsored justice.

Reacting to warlord Yekatom's arrest, anti-Balaka groups threatened to carry out attacks against 'Mission Multidimensionnelle Intégrée des Nations Unies pour la Stabilisation de la République

Centrafricaine' (MINUSCA), NGOs, and civilians in Bossangoa. *Insecurity and mass violence* continued to dominate domestic politics. In a village close to Bossangoa, an incident of mass rape committed by armed men against 17 women on 17 February was made public by 'Médecins Sans Frontières'. Bossangoa was not the only hotspot of violence, although nationally, the number of civilian deaths declined significantly, according to the UN (2017: 1,571; 2018: 697).

Security in *Bangui* remained a source of concern, with heightened tensions in April and May. On 23 February, three people were killed when two rival armed groups shot at each other in the PK5 neighbourhood. Reacting to frequent attacks, MINUSCA, operating jointly with national security forces, arrested seven individuals on 8 April (but not the sought-after leaders, who managed to escape). In the event, 2 individuals were killed and 45 injured, and 11 peacekeepers were injured. During the following night, a MINUSCA camp close to the presidential residence was attacked, sparking fears of a coup d'état. Two days later, when a MINUSCA patrol came under fire, 1 peacekeeper was killed and 11 injured, and about 30 of the attackers were killed. On 11 April, about 200 people demonstrated outside MINUSCA's headquarters, carrying dead bodies from the earlier confrontation. On 1 May, prominent peace activist Abbé Albert Toungoumale Baba and nine civilians were killed in the Fatima church by a Muslim militia, leading to revenge destructions of several mosques and shops, killing in turn at least three Muslims. Hundreds of houses were burned. With the murder of the general vicar of Bambari by UPC soldiers on 29 June, a social media campaign asking for revenge acts on Muslims was launched.

The year had started with heavy fighting in and around Paoua (*North-West*), where the local armed group 'Révolution et Justice' (RJ), in a rare alliance with anti-Balaka groups, attacked the Séléka splinter group 'Mouvement National pour la Libération de la Centrafrique' (MNLC). Reportedly, the MNLC was supported by men on horseback, indicating support from groups originating in

Chad or Sudan. This early fighting claimed the lives of four civilians and caused over a thousand people to flee their homes. For some time, the MNLC held hostage over 100 civilians from a village close to Paoua. After intervention by MINUSCA and the 'Forces Armées Centrafricaines' (FACA; the national armed forces, still under reform), tensions calmed. However, in Markounda (at the Chadian border), fighting between the RJ and the MNLC again flared, displacing more people. The untarred roads of the area were constantly uncontrolled; in one incident, six travelling national education experts were killed. In October, the bigger former Séléka groups, the 'Front Populaire pour la Renaissance de la Centrafrique' (FPRC) and the 'Mouvement Patriotique pour la Centrafrique' (MPC), along with armed young Muslim men, launched a violent attack on an IDP camp in Batangafo, burning down the camp and killing eleven. From June to August, in neighbouring Nana-Grébizi prefecture, allied MPC and FPRC groups clashed with anti-Balaka groups. The FPRC was accused of looting 15 villages near Mbrès, burning more than 2,000 houses and causing thousands of inhabitants to flee.

Bambari and surrounding areas (in *central CAR*) saw again some of the worst confrontations. The 'Union pour la Paix en Centrafrique' (UPC), the third principal Séléka faction, clashed with anti-Balaka militias, and both parties attacked civilians. In March, anti-Balaka fighters killed 15 civilian Fulani herders. UPC fighters in revenge attacked a church in Seko serving as a shelter, killing an estimated 40 IDPs on 21 March. In May, UPC fighters attacked police, gendarmerie, and international security forces in Bambari, leading to massive displacements. In November, UPC commandos also kidnapped several community leaders to prevent young Muslims from being recruited to the FACA. On 15 November, the UPC attacked an IDP camp in Alindao, claiming (potentially rightly so) that it was a safe haven for anti-Balaka elements. They burned down a church, killing at least 70 individuals, among them 2 priests. Around Ippy, intense competition over natural resources and trade routes caused frequent clashes between UPC and anti-Balaka militias.

In *south-eastern CAR*, on 20 January a local anti-Balaka leader, Bere Bere, surrendered to MINUSCA, but this did not ease tensions. In Bangassou, anti-Balaka militias blocked the access of humanitarian organisations to IDPs who had sought refuge at the Catholic mission the previous year. The situation improved only after a delegation of religious leaders from Bangui, led by Cardinal Dieudonné Nzapalainga and Imam Omar Kobine Layama, on 9 April negotiated a preliminary agreement with local militias, civil society, and local authorities. A major offensive by FPRC on the mining town of Bakouma on the last day of the old year ended with the looting of the city; 18,000 residents fled, and dozens were killed in the following period. Anti-Balaka groups frequently harassed MINUSCA convoys. On 17 May, a peacekeeper was killed and 8 injured, while 40 anti-Balaka fighters lost their lives. MINUSCA resorted for a while to air supply for urgent materials. Also in this zone, Fulani families came under attack; in one incident on 20 October, north of Zémio, 5 women and 12 children were killed.

North-eastern CAR also had its share of violence, with protests after the arrest of anti-Balaka leader 'Ramazani' on 16 March in Bria; tensions rose again from August. More than 30 civilians (including 12 women and 2 children) were killed, and more than 44,000 newly displaced people arrived in Bria's PK3 IDP camp, following clashes between FPRC and anti-Balaka groups. FPRC reportedly burned eleven villages south of Bria in order to impose illegal cattle taxation.

A number of more recently created and smaller armed movements also provoked some chaos in the *western part* of the country. In Mambéré-Kadéï and Nana-Mambéré prefectures, the Fulani-backed 'Siriri' group engaged in cattle theft and illegal taxation; it operated from a village in Cameroon. On 22 April, it lost five combatants, including its leader, in an attack on a MINUSCA patrol. In November, the somewhat better organised 'Retour, Réclamation et Réhabilitation' (3R), with a similar ethnic background, disarmed many 'Siriri' fighters. '3R' tried to establish alliances with other armed groups in order to coordinate their grip on the lucrative cattle market. UPC leader Darassa and MPC leader al-Khatim themselves owned thousands of cattle. It became ever clearer that 'Siriri', '3R', and UPC had transformed from 'protectors' of Fulani cattle herders to their 'oppressors', as a report by the UN Group of Experts had it, with traditional Fulani authorities losing power and income to armed movements.

Instead of the one overarching peace agreement that many international actors wanted to see materialise at all costs, it looked as if local agreements, whether on ceasefires or disarmament, would be more effective and realistic. Such agreements were signed in the first quarter of the year in Bangassou, Batangafo, Bouar, and Bria. However, some claims of success were premature. The UN claimed that RJ had agreed to disarm fully and to dissolve itself, which was obviously not the case. Reconciliation processes made some progress (e.g., in Markounda and Zémio) and helped to reduce violence in Bambari, if only temporarily. On a higher level, a new round of consultations between the government and the 14 recognised armed groups took place between February and April: In May, President Touadéra established a committee of 15 advisers to examine their demands and grievances as a basis for future dialogue. Many aspects of that process looked absurd, including the choice of the armed groups, some of which had for years barely been active; others were obviously uninterested in peace.

Both the FPRC and the UPC retained their large zones of influence and claimed to represent the (endangered) Muslim minority (in UPC's case, more particularly the Fulani community). Various demonstrations were organised in Bambari, Bria, Kaga-Bandoro, and Ndélé. The FPRC tried to reunite the Séléka coalition of 2013 that had fallen apart in 2014, but with few tangible results. At a meeting in Moyenne-Sido (at the Chadian border) on 5 August, the three leaders Abdoulaye Hissène (FPRC), Ali Darassa (UPC), and Mahamat al-Khatim (MPC) signed an agreement to organise a 'mixed force' to control transhumance corridors. This was the only moment of unity. One should not forget that FPRC and MPC had earlier clashed in Ndélé (June), killing 'several' people – as many as 30, according to various reports. At the same time, it looked increasingly unlikely that state administration would control the entire eastern half of the country in the foreseeable future, despite some symbolic progress, including, in August, the nomination of five new prefects, including three women, to replace the retired prefects of Bamingui-Bangoran, Basse-Kotto, Mbomou, Nana-Grébizi, and Nana-Mambéré. Some of the armed movements, certainly the bigger ones, managed to solidly pursue their parallel economic activities, exploiting and smuggling natural resources, as well as taxing traders at illegal checkpoints. Parallel to this, intercommunal tensions increased, fuelled by sectarian rhetoric.

MINUSCA's response to this state of affairs was rather defensive. It reinforced positions south of Kaga-Bandoro to prevent armed group movement towards Bangui, but it also occasionally used air strikes against FPRC vehicles seeking to bypass checkpoints.

Compared to earlier years (and to other armed groups), the *Lord's Resistance Army* caused only limited havoc. Twelve attacks on villages were recorded, as were 38 abductions.

Foreign Affairs

President Touadéra, in line with positions taken earlier by some government ministers, called for the integral lifting of the UNSC's *arms embargo* on 4 October. This stood in the context of Russian arms deliveries to FACA agreed in late 2017. *Russian influence* gained in importance, with President Touadéra relying on Russian services also for his own security. An important shipment of arms from Russia was recorded on 27 January, and in the following months, an estimated 300–400 Russian specialists were deployed, mostly to help FACA reconquer terrain. In July, three Russian journalists – working for a media outlet owned by Mikhaïl Khodorkovski, an exiled opponent to Russian president Putin – were killed on the Dekoa-Sibut axis by armed men. The circumstances were not fully established, but it was obvious that the journalists had been investigating the engagement of the Russian private security company Wagner, owned by a close confidant of the Russian president. An official investigation was launched, and the Russian security advisor to Touadéra, Valery Zakharov, qualified the killings as criminal acts. On 22 August, both countries signed a defence agreement. Some observers compared Zakharov to the dreaded French colonel Mantion who had decisive influence over former President Kolingba (1981–93). Zakharov allegedly pushed Touadéra to seek the dismissal of parliament speaker Meckassoua.

Increasing Russian influence was not appreciated by more traditional partners of CAR, in particular France. According to 'Jeune Afrique', French president Emmanuel Macron used the opportunity of the OIF summit in Armenia on 1 October to warn Touadéra about growing Russian influence, supported in this by subregional heads of state Déby (Chad), Sassou Nguesso (Congo), and Bongo (Gabon). Paris may have been driven by the impulse to preserve its influence, but a more neutral position would concur that the Russian arms deliveries to FACA incited a new arms race in the subregion (with small arms coming from Chad, Congo, and Sudan), and also risked reconfiguring rebel group alliances. *France*, for its part, maintained around 50 military trainers and tactical drones in CAR. On 2 November, French foreign minister Jean-Yves Le Drian announced military aid worth € 24 m and arms deliveries (1,400 assault rifles), obviously in an attempt to counterbalance Russian moves.

The arrest of anti-Balaka leader Patrice-Edouard Ngaïssona in Paris on 12 December was a noticeable event. The arrest warrant for alleged war crimes and crimes against humanity (just like with Yekatom) against the "National General Coordinator" of the anti-Balaka movement had been issued only five days earlier. Ngaïssona, a former sports minister, had managed to get elected to the board of the Confederation of African Football (CAF) at a meeting in Morocco on 2 February, in spite of allegations that he had been responsible for atrocities during the civil war. Despite his arrest, Ngaïssona's wing of the anti-Balaka movement remained part of the overall peace process. In protest against the arrest of Ngaïssona, the other important faction of the anti-Balaka movement (led by Maxime Mokom) issued a communiqué in which it announced its withdrawal from the national disarmament, repatriation, and reintegration process (though without much consequence).

An *African Initiative for Peace and Reconciliation* under the aegis of the AU had been the framework of consultations already in late 2017. Its panel of facilitators concluded a listening tour with the 14 'main' armed groups and submitted a consolidated list of grievances and priorities of those groups to President Touadéra for consideration by the government. This procedure was criticised by civil society, members of parliament, and other stakeholders for a lack of inclusiveness. They resented the sidelining of civilians and victims from the peace process. Opposition political parties and civil society organisations issued a joint memorandum on 12 November calling for their inclusion in the process. The absurdity of including on the same footing the three most important Séléka factions, a number of fragmented groups with unclear hierarchies, and also groups with at best local influence was complemented by the incoherence of keeping individuals under sanctions at the same time as courting them. However, this was partly due to a parallel process that risked undermining the AU-led mediation. Under joint Russian and Sudanese initiative, important meetings with former Séléka leaders were held in Khartoum (on 10 July and 18 August) – theoretically, and according to the sanctions regime, FPRC leaders Nourredine Adam and Abdoulaye Hissène should not have been allowed to travel.

The *UN* institutions fully supported the AU-led peace initiative. Touadéra attended a high-level meeting of the Peacebuilding Commission and one convened by the president of the UNGA on peacebuilding and sustaining peace (24–25 April) in New York. António Guterres (UNSG), Touadéra, Moussa Faki Mahamat (chairman of the AU commission), and Ahmad Allam-Mi (CEEAC secretary general) co-chaired a further high-level ministerial meeting on the margins of the seventy-third session of the UNGA on 27 September. On 15 November, the UNSC renewed MINUSCA's mandate for a further 13 months and by a separate resolution on 3 December extended that mandate. Facing enormous security challenges, popular anger, and criticism from the government, MINUSCA looked overburdened, on top of which, nine new allegations of serious misconduct, including sexual exploitation and abuse, were made public. The EU Training Mission, operating in CAR since July 2016 and claiming to have trained 3,400 FACA soldiers, saw its mandate extended on 30 July to 19 September 2020.

Socioeconomic Developments

The EIU, estimated *GDP growth*, after quite difficult years, at 4.3%, which looked rather positive, while, however, it indicated the consumer price inflation at a rather high 6%. The IMF, pursuing its fiscal reform programme, reviewed the country's *ECF agreement* and approved a disbursement of $ 32.1 m in July, despite acknowledging high risks, including debt distress (and ongoing violence). The fiscal deficit was estimated at 2.1% of GDP, and the government continued to rely on donors, particularly as the National Assembly did not approve increases in taxes on forestry and diamond exports, the export economy's two most important sectors.

It was quite difficult to draw an exact picture of *diamond production and export*. Quantities given by the UN (based on government figures) and by the Kimberley Process report varied, but the bulk of official exports was from stockpiles. Government income from diamond exports was only around $ 10 m. At the same time, a former Séléka officer and presidential advisor was dismissed from his position after a video released on social media showed him marketing diamonds at his home (29 August). Delays in giving clearance to exports under the Kimberley Process monitoring system had detrimental effects on legal ways to export gems as this forced most buying house to close office. Diamond smuggling grew as artisanal miners and collectors had no other option. In contrast, legal *gold* production and exports grew, but here as well most of the gold was believed to leave the country illegally. Most production sites were under rebel control, which did not mean that gold from those sites would automatically be sold illegally (in the absence of a comparable process to the Kimberley Protocol), which led the UN expert group to conclude that "legal trade in gold … contributes … to the financing of armed groups". Three Chinese employees of a gold mining company were killed on 4 October following strong tensions between local and foreign mining operators.

Forced displacement continued to haunt society. By midyear about 573,000 CAR citizens were refugees in neighbouring countries – an increase of 43,000 compared to 2017. Worse still was the increase to up to 674,000 in the number of IDPs, exceeding 2014 records. Considering that IDP camps and health centres were regularly targeted by violent attacks, the conditions in such centres were life-threatening. Female IDPs and children were hardest hit. 'Médecins Sans Frontières' claimed to treat an average of 300 survivors of rape and sexual assault per month, mostly in Bangui.

The socioeconomic picture was, however, only complete when considering the ongoing *humanitarian crisis*. According to OCHA, 63% of the population were in need of humanitarian assistance and protection, 1.3 m were in need of shelter, and around 50% had no access to safe drinking water. Put in different terms, 3 m lived in extreme poverty, with 43% of the population affected by food insecurity. One child in three suffered from severe malnutrition – a sad balance sheet in a country where, given the climatic conditions, agriculture should be able to feed the entire population. Obviously, generalised insecurity was a main factor of this dismal situation. As a consequence, CAR was second to last on the HDI. The UN found it hard to attract assistance. While the Humanitarian Response Plan requested $ 515.6 m, it received only $ 254.9 m (49%). According to the UN, CAR was also one of the deadliest humanitarian contexts in the world. During the year, aid workers abandoned Kabo and Markounda, and 6 humanitarian workers were killed and 23 injured, while a total of 396 security incidents against humanitarian actors were recorded, and 25 of 137 registered organisations suspended their operations.

Select Bibliography on Central African Republic

Books and Refereed Journal Articles, 2009–2020

Working papers and reports are not included in this bibliography.

Bagayoko, Niagalé (2012) 'Multilevel governance and security: security sector reform in the Central African Republic', *IDS Bulletin*, 43 (4), pp. 20–34.

Bono, Giovanna (2011) 'The EU's military operation in Chad and the Central African Republic: an operation to save lives?' *Journal of Intervention and Statebuilding*, 5 (1), pp. 1–21.

Carayannis, Tatiana/Lombard, Louisa (2015) eds. *Making Sense of the Central African Republic*, London: Zed Books, 357 p.

Carayannis, Tatiana/Mignonne Fowlis (2017) 'Lessons from African Union–United Nations cooperation in peace operations in the Central African Republic', *African Security Review*, 26 (2), pp. 220–236.

Chauvin, Emmanuel/Christian Seignobos (2013) 'L'imbroglio centrafricain', *Afrique contemporaine* 248, pp. 119–148.

De Vries, Lotje/Andreas Mehler (2019) 'The limits of instrumentalizing disorder: Reassessing the neopatrimonial perspective in the Central African Republic', *African Affairs*, 118 (471), pp. 307–327.

Filakota, Richard (2009) *Le renouveau islamique en Afrique noire: l'exemple de la Centrafrique,* Paris: L'Harmattan, 2009, 210 p.

Glasius, Marlies (2009) 'We ourselves, we are part of the functioning': the ICC, victims, and civil society in the Central African Republic', *African Affairs*, 108 (430), pp. 49–67.

Glawion, Tim/Lotje De Vries (2018) 'Ruptures revoked: why the Central African Republic's unprecedented crisis has not altered deep-seated patterns of governance.' *The Journal of Modern African Studies,* 56 (3), 421–442.

Glawion, Tim/Lotje de Vries/Andreas Mehler (2019) 'Handle with Care! A Qualitative Comparison of the Fragile States Index's Bottom Three Countries: Central African Republic, Somalia and South Sudan', *Development and Change,* 50 (2), pp. 277–300.

Käihkö, Ilmari/Mats Utas (2014) 'The crisis in CAR: Navigating myths and interests', *Africa Spectrum,* 49 (1), pp. 69–77.

Glawion, Tim (2020) *The Security Arena in Africa: Local Order-Making in the Central African Republic, Somaliland, and South Sudan*, Cambridge: Cambridge University Press.

Lombard, Louisa (2012) 'Rébellion et limites de la consolidation de la paix en République Centrafricaine' *Politique africaine*, 125, pp. 189–208.

Lombard, Louisa (2013) 'Navigational tools for Central African road-blocks', *PoLAR: Political and Legal Anthropology Review,* 36 (1) pp. 157–173.

Lombard, Louisa/Sylvain Batianga-Kinzi (2015) 'Violence, popular punishment, and war in the Central African Republic', *African Affairs,* 114 (454), pp. 52–71.

Lombard, Louisa (2016) *State of rebellion: violence and intervention in the Central African Republic*. London: Zed Books, 300 p.

Lombard, Louisa (2016) 'Threat economies and armed conservation in northeastern Central African Republic', *Geoforum* 69, pp. 218–226.

Lombard, Louisa (2018) 'Denouncing Sovereignty: Claims to Liberty in Northeastern Central African Republic', *Comparative Studies in Society and History,* 60 (4), pp. 1066–1095.

Lombard, Louisa/Enrica Picco (2019) 'Distributive justice at war: displacement and its afterlives in the Central African Republic', *Journal of Refugee Studies*, 1–24.

Marchal, Roland (2009) *Aux marges du monde, en Afrique Centrale*, Paris: CERI (Les études du CERI, 153/154), 50 p.

Mayneri, Andrea Ceriana (2014) 'La Centrafrique, de la rébellion Séléka aux groupes anti-balaka (2012–2014): Usages de la violence, schème persécutif et traitement médiatique du conflit', *Politique africaine,* 137, pp. 179–193.

Mehler, Andreas (2005–2019) 'Central African Republic', *Africa Yearbook (2004–2018)*. *Politics, Economy and Society South of the Sahara*, ed. by Andreas Mehler, Henning Melber and different co-editors, Leiden: Brill 2005–2019.

Mehler, Andreas (2012) 'Why Security Forces Do Not Deliver Security: Evidence from Liberia and the Central African Republic', *Armed Forces and Society*, 38 (1), pp. 46–69.

Mehler, Andreas (2011) 'Rebels and Parties: The Impact of Armed Insurgency on Representation in the Central African Republic', *The Journal of Modern African Studies*, 49 (1), 115–139.

Meyer, Angela (2009) 'Regional conflict management in Central Africa: from FOMUC to MICOPAX, *African Security* 2 (2–3), pp. 158–174.

Thomas, Yanis (2016) *Centrafrique: un destin volé. Histoire d'une domination française.* Paris: Agone/Survie, 235 p.

Vinck, Patrick/Phuong N. Pham (2010), 'Outreach evaluation: The international criminal court in the Central African Republic' *International Journal of Transitional Justice,* 4 (3), pp. 421–442.

Welz, Martin (2014) 'Briefing: Crisis in the Central African Republic and the international response', *African Affairs*, 113 (453), pp. 601–610.

Welz, Martin (2016) 'Multi-actor peace operations and inter-organizational relations: insights from the Central African Republic', *International Peacekeeping,* 23 (4), pp. 568–591.

Printed in the United States
by Baker & Taylor Publisher Services